THE
FAMILY
GARDEN

——

THE
FAMILY
GARDEN

Creating Safe and Attractive Areas for All to Enjoy

Pamela Allardice

Angus&Robertson

An imprint of HarperCollins*Publishers*

TO GREG, EDWARD AND RANDALL

Acknowledgements

The author and publisher wish to thank the following for their kind permission to reproduce material in this book:

Page 107 *Gardens for Children,* Tigger Wise; Kangaroo Press, 1986

Angus & Robertson
Angus&Robertson, an imprint of HarperCollins*Publishers*

First published in Australia in 1995

HarperCollins*Publishers*
25 Ryde Road, Pymble, Sydney NSW 2073, Australia
31 View Road, Glenfield, Auckland 10, New Zealand
77–85 Fulham Palace Road, London W6 8JB, United Kingdom
Hazelton Lanes, 55 Avenue Road, Suite 2900, Toronto, Ontario M5R 3L2
and 1995 Markham Road, Scarborough, Ontario M1B 5M8, Canada
10 East 53rd Street, New York NY 10032, USA

National Library of Australia Cataloguing-in-Publication data:

Allardice, Pamela, 1958- .
The family garden.
Includes index.

ISBN 0 207 17856 9.
1. Gardening. 2. Gardens – Design. I. Title.
635

Designed by Michelle Wiener
Colour illustrations by Karen Carter
Black-and-white illustrations by Russell Jeffery

Printed in Hong Kong
9 8 7 6 5 4 3 2 1   99 98 97 96 95

CONTENTS

Plants softly trailing over the top of this retaining wall of pine logs of uneven heights gives the garden a softer, more natural look

1

GROUND RULES

_____

Fences, Hedges and Walls

All gardens will need some sort of construction, whether it is simply laying a path, or more complicated tasks, such as siting a driveway or erecting fences or walls.

Within a large garden, walls or fences can be ornamental rather than functional, separating, say, a vegetable garden or a 'secret' walled courtyard garden from the rest of the garden. Even on a very small scale, they can be used effectively to screen a utility area, such as a compost heap. Hedges, especially, can be used to divide up a garden quite subtly and, if you have the space, you can even screen the fence itself with a hedge, creating a long alley suitable for storing gardening equipment and other household items.

Most commonly, however, discussion about fences, hedges or walls concerns the definition of a garden's boundaries; their primary objective is to protect the garden and give some measure of privacy to the inhabitants. They may also be designed to a height and style that will keep children and dogs confined — or keep them out — and provide shelter from wind, noise and dust. Depending on the aspect, you might plan for a fence to provide support for creepers or vines or, in a more formal garden, something like espaliered camellias or fruit trees.

If you are planning to grow closely foliaged shrubs or vines over a fence or wall, consider

incorporating one or two bird feeders as well, provided they can be placed out of reach of cats. Birds will find the tangle of vines a safe nesting place, particularly if they are encouraged to stop there for food. As well as softening the fence line, climbing plants can provide an often much-needed splash of colour. Most will need supports or lattice for tendrils to twine around. Either string wire or twine along the fence at regular intervals or purchase green plastic-covered wire which may be stapled or nailed to the fence. For a fence that catches sunshine most of the day, try a bright bougainvillea or Chinese star jasmine, with its small white flowers and glossy green leaves. A slightly cooler aspect would favour the glorious orange-flowered 'Chinese Fingers' or one of the honeysuckles, such as *Lonicera brownii* 'Firecracker'.

It is very important to first consult with local council authorities. Front, side and back fences are all governed by different laws and there are many regulations regarding their height and access by utility service personnel. In some areas, notably those developed in the late 1950s and early 1960s, front fences were outlawed in favour of planting shrubs and trees. It is a relatively easy matter to overcome this particular covenant, but it will require agreement from neighbours. Side fences are governed by similar laws, requiring neighbours to negotiate on the placement of the

A picket fence suits an older-style timber cottage

fence and its cost. When planning the siting of your fence, consider the placement of any existing trees near the boundaries. A very simple trick to create design interest and also to create an illusion of space and depth is to carry a fence line around a tree. Alternatively, a tree may be planted in a deliberately created indentation. This is a terrific idea for a narrow front boundary fence as it can make the block seem wider.

The shape of a garden is defined by its boundaries but the effect within the garden is determined by the type of walls or fences used. For instance, a stained or broken brick wall can quickly be turned into an asset with a coat of white paint, helping to create a fresh, light mood in the garden and to throw plants into relief. In small city gardens especially, the fence or wall can become an essential design component. Luxuriant planting of ivy can focus the eye inwards towards the peace of the garden rather than outwards, towards the hustle and bustle.

This feeling can be accentuated with the addition of a small shady pool or statuette.

Fences and walls may be constructed from an enormous variety of materials, depending on climatic conditions and, of course, personal taste. Dry stone walls, rustic post-and-rail fences, formal wrought-iron or decorative galvanised wire fences, plain stone or tinted or decoratively rendered cement blocks along with the ever-popular picket fence are all possible choices. When we were living in Melbourne, we were in an old house that had a corrugated iron fence. Such fences were once quite common in old worker's cottages, but are now seldom built new. If you have one, soften its rather bald appearance with climbers or dense shrubs — I used May bushes — and paint it green to blend with the garden. Metal fences are not the best choice for a family garden as they can buckle and split; the resulting torn edges will rust and present a danger to children. Whatever material you favour, the general rule of thumb for fencing is that it should complement the style and period of the house.

The picket fence is particularly popular with families renovating older timber cottages and Federation or 'Queen Anne' style homes. A picket fence is a pretty and appropriate choice for a decorative front fence to complement a dainty cottage garden; herbs and old-fashioned favourites like geraniums and pinks can be encouraged to peek through the pickets in a most appealing fashion. Picket fences come in a wide variety of designs with different cut-out motifs, such as hearts, circles and diamonds. Such fences can be features in themselves or can be used as a frame for densely-planted flower beds. Picket fences are simple enough to be constructed by an experienced home renovating or building enthusiast. Important points to remember are: the pickets should be kept clear of the soil; the horizontal rails should be cut with an outward slope so rain does not run down the vertical posts as much, and pickets should be placed reasonably close together to avoid a gap-toothed look.

Simpler timber fences, constructed from hardwood, cedar, treated pine, or redwood, are another option and can look most appropriate with a modern home that incorporates natural materials, and with a garden which features native plants that enjoy wind movement rather than shelter. These fences can be painted a dull green or dark brown or left to weather naturally so they blend with the garden. The slats may be arranged in such a way as to create an interesting feature, as well as redirect wind flow. Horizontal slats, or those angled at 45 degrees, will help scatter wind flow; more privacy may be created in living or relaxation areas by overlapping the slats, blocking wind access.

Simplest of all is the ubiquitous Australian backyard fence of hardwood palings. There is no need for these to be dull, though; plan to cover them with pretty creepers, or even choko vines, and consider some of the newer styles which feature a lattice trim on the top for extra height and privacy. These have the advantage of filtering wind flow into the garden rather than

A plain wooden paling fence can be enhanced by painting it to blend with the garden

creating a build-up of turbulence at head level, which can occur in unprotected hillside gardens.

If you are looking for something different from a paling fence, tea-tree, brush or sapling fences add a little extra interest and harmonise well with plants and climbers to produce a pleasantly integrated rustic look, even in a very new garden. Brushwood fences are probably one of the most ancient forms of fencing. Archaeologists tell us that early people would encircle their huts with pieces of thorny brush to deter animals. Brushwood fences are an easy and durable method of home fencing. Commercially harvested and dried brushwood can be purchased ready-cut and fastened between purchased metal posts and clipped onto wire struts, according to the manufacturer's instructions, by any reasonably competent home renovating or building enthusiast. Simple fences like this are often seen in the mountain-top villages of Papua New Guinea and other isolated

There are many alternatives to the paling fence, such as this one made of bamboo

spots, and they work just as well in the family garden. With either a brushwood or sapling fence it is important to ensure both the footings and the capping boards are sound, otherwise they will warp and eventually topple over.

An unusual option is the wicket fence, a traditional type of fencing made by weaving young green branches, strips of pliable timber or even heavy vines between timber uprights. This is the forerunner to the modern commercially prepared lattice and can form an arresting feature in a garden, particularly when used as a base for a lush tropical-style vine, such as a pink-flowered *Pandorea jasminoides*. Of course, modern timber lattice can also be used for fencing. This is usually made from treated pine and may be painted or, more commonly, left to weather to a pleasant grey-green. It is also possible to buy lattice made from fibrecement sheets, in which square or diamond-shaped holes have been punched. This type of fencing is more durable than timber but is possibly not as visually appealing. It would, however, be an excellent choice for a seaside garden where salt air rapidly weathers almost everything.

Quality masonry or stone and iron fences with elegant bronze letterboxes and bellpulls look marvellous with the rather more grand Victorian homes. Stucco is a slightly less

expensive option and just as historically accurate. Wrought-iron fences were very popular during the late Victorian period and were often used in conjunction with decorative wrought-iron balconies and in-fills on inner city terrace houses. Rust was, however, always a problem with this type of fencing. Modern reproduction wrought-iron fencing is usually made from white or green powder-coated galvanised iron or steel tubes, topped with Victorian style spearheads or clubs.

Stone or brick fences can be either solid or built with regular gaps, later to be filled in with decorative cast-iron palings or timber pickets. This style creates a 'lighter' look without jeopardising security, and can be more proportionate to a medium-sized family home. This sort of fence will allow for wind moderation and dispersal, whereas a solid fence can actually create the turbulence referred to earlier. It is important to choose bricks that will match the house.

Brick fences can be painted, which can create an attractive foil for plants, especially if the paint is white or grey. Another option much favoured in European courtyards is to incorporate inserts — either ornamental tiles or patterns created by decoratively arranging the bricks.

Even though a high-quality stone or brick

A stone and iron fence complements a formal style of house and garden

fence will require substantial investment, it cannot be bettered for durability and should have a life of many decades. It is most important that it be well-constructed. The home building enthusiast can construct brick walls if great care is taken with spirit levels and measurements, however, it is likely to be an expensive experiment, so it is probably best to enlist professional help to determine the footings and the setting out of the fence. Single brick walls, if they are on the longish side, must be supported approximately every 2 metres by a built-in pier or buttress. If the wall is completely freestanding, the bricklayer must allow for regular vertical expansion joints for the whole height of the wall. A stable foundation trench for a masonry fence should be excavated to at least 1 metre, so care must be taken to avoid digging up telephone wires, gas pipes and electricity cables. For continuous high brick fences, the footings should be made from

reinforced concrete. If you plan to grow plants or foliage over the wall, discuss this with your bricklayer. Extra metal rods should be incorporated into any wall that is going to bear the additional weight of vines; similarly, metal supports for a pull-out laundry line or frame should ideally be built into a brick wall rather than just attached later.

I would love to have stone walls in my garden. Old blocks of local stones, like sandstone, bluestone or limestone, give a garden a timeless atmosphere and are also very long-lasting — witness the centuries-old stone walls found on English farms, usually made by the farmer collecting together large stones from the immediate area. Stone walls can be left rough-surfaced, encouraging the growth of attractive lichens and mosses, or they can be cut and polished along more formal lines.

The traditional stone walls of England were, as their name suggests, built by carefully fitting

rocks on top of each other; any gaps between them were filled with gravel and, eventually, pockets of flowers would grow. Flat sections of sandstone, slate or bluestone are probably the easiest to use for constructing a dry stone wall, or 'dry-walling'. Shards of softer stones, such as basalt or pumice may weather more quickly than the other harder stones. Importantly, the base of the wall should be at least twice as wide as the anticipated width of its top course, for stability's sake. The base stones should be set into a base of sand and gravel. Plants such as Black-Eyed Susans or *Viola hederacea* will grow well in soil placed in the cracks of a dry stone wall; alternatively, try your luck by just scattering seed all over the wall and seeing what comes up.

Also common today are stonework fences, either constructed from rubble or other irregular stones set into mortar. Slate breaks along natural lines to form flat shapes and these can be used to 'face' either rough brickwork or angled concrete retaining walls. Examples of these 'stone' walls

A well-constructed stone wall is both durable and attractive

can be seen in many public parks and it is an easy enough technique to copy. Dressed stone masonry, however, is best left to experienced masons, particularly when it comes to installing hingeposts and gates.

Wire fences, made from mass-produced interlocked patterns of steel wire or chain wire, first became popular during the 1920s and 1930s in Australia. Before that, wire fences were mainly erected around labourers' houses in the early 1880s, but with mechanisation came fancy designs and wire scrollwork, which became popular in the new suburbs. Along with more ornate Victorian cast-iron fences, many wire fences were bundled up and smelted to produce scrap metal during the Second World War. Now, with the interest in renovating older homes 'true to period', many manufacturers are producing wire fences again.

Wire fencing was — and is still — relatively cheap and easy to erect. The fencing is nailed to iron star posts or treated timber struts. They are mostly used with low brick plinths or squat brick piers as a base. Some of the newer steel mesh or heavy gauge welded mesh fences can support a dense cover of climbing plants. A house in our neighbourhood has a sturdy wire mesh fence covered with *Wisteria sinensis* (too heavy and grasping for most other support materials) and a pink hardenbergia — pretty as well as practical and economical.

A foliage-draped fence is closely related to a plant-based screen or 'living fence' — the hedge. The important difference between fences or walls and hedges is that, although they will provide an equal measure of privacy and even temperature control, they are less likely to contain children or pets. Almost any shrub or tree, or combination of both, can be used to make a beautiful barrier. The English box and cypress pine have been widely used for this purpose, their only drawback being that both can take years to reach a practical height. *Abelia* and *Murraya* species are faster growing with the bonus of sweetly scented flowers for passersby to enjoy. Australian natives, such as *Boronia megastigma* and mintbush (*Prostanthera ovalifolia*) can be clipped to

Things to Do

Children are not noted for their patience, so they will find growing mustard and cress — the fastest crop of all — very satisfying. It is also fun for children who do not have access to a garden, for mustard and cress will grow on newspaper, cloth or absorbent paper.

Take a shallow foil or plastic tray and cover the base with cotton wool, towelling or absorbent paper; wet this thoroughly. Sow the seed thickly, then put the tray in a shady place for a day or two. When the seeds have sprouted, put the tray in full light and, when the little plants are about 6 centimetres high, they may be snipped off with scissors and used whole or chopped on sandwiches or in salads — delicious! Sow seed every ten to 14 days for a continuous supply.

produce a lovely hedge. You could also consider blending foliage within a hedge to create interest and contrast. Planting banks of different lavenders — say, purple, pink, and the tiny white *Lavandula angustifolia* 'Alba' — can create a lusciously scented hedge that responds well to regular pruning.

It is important that whichever plant or plants you select for a hedge, they must have the ability to shoot easily after each trimming. A hedge should be trimmed regularly to maintain the desired height and thickness. Regular feeding is also very important and will help prevent dieback in the core of the hedge. Try to avoid using prickly shrubs or those with poisonous sap or berries; a child or a pet taking a short cut through a hedge could easily come to grief.

Attractive Edgings

Most garden designs will incorporate different shaped areas for different functions, for example, lawns, garden beds, utility areas, pathways and patios. Sturdy and attractive edgings are necessary both for aesthetic and practical reasons. Edgings can contribute to visual and spatial harmony in the garden by separating and defining the layout. What is probably more important, though, is that without edge strips or gutters, lawn grass would quickly invade garden beds, and brickwork or pavers would begin to loosen around the edges.

When deciding where edge strips or low gutters will go, make sure you have allowed for adequate water flow. If you are using concrete edgings, ensure they are angled so that water will not puddle in beds or on paths. Various edgings can be used, the simplest being a lawn edge trimmed to a neat border where it meets with a garden bed. Reinforced concrete edging is a widespread choice for council kerb and guttering work because it best facilitates water flow. There are a number of variations on this method which can be used in the garden itself: precast concrete edging blocks can be set into a base of mortar; concrete can actually be cast into place around the area to be edged or fancy bricks or pavers can be mortared to a flat sheet of concrete. Concrete edging is definitely the most appropriate method for a patio or pathway; if

the bricks or pavers are just laid on sand then, even with only light usage, they will eventually shift and become dangerous.

Concrete may be used to construct standard garden bed edges. This is a relatively easy method to learn and most gardeners will soon be able to make all the garden edges and gutters they need for their garden. You can even cast your own concrete edging blocks, and how about adding a yellow pigment (about 5 kilograms of oxide pigment will colour one cubic metre of concrete) and creating a 'Yellow Brick Road' to trail enticingly around the borders of your plants? Simple, lightweight concrete edgings can be made by pouring the mixture into an old plastic ice cream container to a depth of 4 centimetres. When set, they may either be used flat as pavers, or inserted into shallow trenches, level with the bricks or pavers or the garden bed, or they can be concealed by dropping them slightly below the surface. Alternatively, a trench-style foundation can be prepared, then bricks or pavers can be laid directly on a layer of mortar, or the concrete can be left exposed as a mower strip.

If you are feeling creative, concrete edgings do not have to be boring. You can trim the surface with a mixture of finely crushed sandstone or granite to give an interesting finish, or add texture by brushing patterns into the concrete by 'sweeping' it with a stiff wire brush. Most pleasing of all, just leave a few gaps in the

Tip

Keen gardeners will avoid much heartache if they accept that children are naturally destructive in a garden. They like plants that they can actually *do* something with, rather than just look at. So, be aware that fuchsia buds are satisfying to pop, and plant a lot if you want them as a cut flower for the house as well; also that snapdragon heads are liable to be used as finger puppets and that the fat pink flowers of *Grevillea longifolia* will be used as 'toothbrushes'!

edging and allow a bit of greenery to spill out.

The easiest way to purchase concrete is to order it from a ready-mix concrete supplier. Check the telephone directory and look for a supplier who provides 'mini-crete' trucks, especially for use by home gardeners. These little mixers only hold the relatively small amount of concrete usually ordered for a job on an average suburban lot.

Brickwork is a popular choice for constructing garden edgings. An old-fashioned method much favoured by cottage garden enthusiasts is to simply stand bricks or half-bricks on their edges in a straight or curved line. It is not advisable to just lay bricks flat as they seldom look attractive this way. Firstly, estimate how many bricks you will require to fill in the line or curve you want. Stretch string between pegs to indicate where the edging will go, then dig out a narrow trench and pack bricks firmly against the inside edge. Spread a little mortar along the bottom of the trench to hold the bricks

Edgings between garden beds and lawn are necessary for both practical and aesthetic reasons

tightly in position before soil is pressed firmly against them. It is usually a good idea to run another strip of mortar along the base of the outside of the bricks to finish off.

Short wooden logs held firmly in position can be used to create durable edging strips. It is, however, vital to ensure all such timber has been treated to repel insects — particularly termites — and fungi. Durable timbers to look for include jarrah, river red gum and ironbark; treated pine is a relatively inexpensive alternative. Old railway sleepers can be recycled successfully as garden edgings. They can also be used easily to create various levels in the garden and produce retaining walls. Treated pine logs can be built up, crisscross fashion, and secured with purchased weatherproof log clamps to make excellent retaining walls. Another idea is to drill holes in the ends of the logs and bolt or rope them together with weatherproof fixing.

Timber edgings and treated logs give a lovely natural appearance to a garden, blending particularly well with ferns and native plants. More decorative terracotta or Victorian-style curved wire edgings are better suited to formal display beds or courtyards. Tiny, white-painted picket edging can be delightful alongside a sunny little path or around a bright bed of geraniums or petunias. However, be wary of the stake-pointed type in the family garden, which could spell disaster for a romping child who suddenly trips and falls.

Stonework makes an effective and attractive edging. Either use dry-packed stones and pebbles to create a miniature version of a dry stone wall (see pages 13–14) or join stones together with mortar. Slate, sandstone, limestone, granite and marble can all be used, but professional advice should be sought prior to assembling the edges as some varieties of the different stones are more vulnerable to weathering and snapping than others. 'Bush' rocks are usually blue-grey basalt or golden shades of sandstone and may be purchased from reputable suppliers. Their colour and texture will complement most garden designs. Making stonework edgings and paths can be likened to joining together pieces from a jigsaw puzzle. A good tip to remember is to go for a weaker, rather than stronger, mortar mix. That way, if you make a mistake or see a spot where a piece can be more attractively placed as you work your way along, it is easier to remove, clean and re-bed the individual stones. When selecting stones, ask for those that have been split along natural lines rather than sawn or cut; this means they will wear better.

Steps

Steps are a functional way of connecting different levels in your garden. Somewhere in the garden you are likely to require a step or two and, even if your land is not sloping, from a design point of view, steps can provide a structural break from unrelieved horizontal lines. In fact, introducing an artificial slope and a small flight of steps is often a simple way to create a focal point in a garden and to invite further exploration — even if they only lead to a compost bin or toolshed!

Steps should always be wide enough for safe use by children and the elderly. The ideal height for every step is about 175 millimetres and the width, from front to back, 275 millimetres. However, steps should also relate to the 'feel' and size of the garden. For instance, in a tiny area you may find that only a low shelf is required, while in a larger space quite ambitious flights of steps, flanked by stepped beds of flowers, could well be incorporated into retaining walls without disrupting the visual harmony. With a large flight of steps, always consider the view you will have as you walk up and down. To accentuate aspects of the garden you might like to experiment with a gorgeous specimen tree, like

Rough wooden steps overgrown with ivy create an interesting effect

Magnolia stellata, which only becomes visible as you climb or descend the steps. Or, consider a carefully placed pond or rock garden that hugs the side of the steps and may be enjoyed as the steps are climbed. Often stepped beds alongside the treads provide a gardening bonus, making it possible to plant lime-loving and lime-hating plants side by side to create imaginative 'hanging garden' effects.

When setting out the steps, remember that rhythm is critical to safety. Put simply, steps with small risers and wide, flat treads are easiest to walk up and down; also, the risers should be equal and the distances between the treads should allow adequate space and be easy to reach when walking. Although on long gentle slopes treads need not be vertical, it is sensible to ensure that all treads are the same to reduce the risk of stumbling, and to start and end steps on safe, flat areas, making them flush with upper and lower lawn or path areas.

You should consider handrails or supports

when installing a set of steps. With short or gently sloping steps this may not be an issue, but a good, strong, continuous handrail is a must if the steps are to be used by the elderly or infirm or, for that matter, by children. Metal or timber handrails are usually the more practical and cost-efficient option. Decorative picket or wire fencing along a flight of steps can look pretty but will doubtless be more expensive. A wide range of attractive, soft-foliaged plants can be positioned alongside the handrail to soften its appearance. For a long flight of steps you might also like to incorporate a resting place halfway — a cut-off stump or flat, sunwarmed rock can be placed to the side of the steps for rest or contemplation. A single step dividing two levels of lawn can present just as attractive an opportunity to create a welcome rest area — a small slender tree with a stone or timber bench beneath it, surrounded by small flowering ground covers or low shrubs can create a delightful accent in a garden.

Wide steps with low risers will create a mood conducive to a leisurely stroll through a garden. Drifts of creeping plants and groundcovers can be planted alongside to further soften the edges of the steps. Steep steps, on the other hand, are best placed where their use is unavoidable, perhaps in a small garden where a more sprawling arrangement would encroach too much on any flat area. Steep steps are also a must to cope with a sharp slope in the garden — grass is not always the best solution as soil erosion can cause a patchy effect which is dangerous when wet.

Many beautiful old gardens incorporate a formal series of stone or brick steps, topped with a gracious balustrade and ascending in a semicircle to a patio or to the house itself. Other step materials, such as wooden sleepers, stone flags or bush rocks blend best with relaxed bush, tropical, or cottage style gardens. Remember the shape of a flight of steps can also influence the atmosphere in the garden. A dramatic impact can be created with assymetrical concrete or

Wooden steps wind their way through a natural setting in a garden

Concrete steps edged with pieces of recycled timber are simple to construct. Drill holes through the ends of the timber and hammer reinforcing rods through the holes to hold the timber in place. Fill the area between the pieces of timber with concrete. Ensure that the timber surrounds do not become too damp and slippery.

marble blocks, set at a bold gradient.

Depending on the severity of the slope — wide, straight steps are excellent for short slopes — such an arrangement can present an exciting opportunity for a feature. Curved steps are more suited to longer slopes. The prettiest examples of curved steps are often to be seen in country gardens where informal steps wind their way between flower beds and around grassy banks, leaving the slope between the steps free for trailing groundcover plants. Stone slabs cut into an existing slope and set at regular intervals, are an easy way to build steps in an informal garden.

Simple timber steps, made from either railway sleepers or treated round logs, can lend a rustic appeal. To ensure a snug fit, cut the step base into the slope and then cut or saw the timber or stone to fit. If using timber, some sort of preservative should be applied to prevent rotting. Avoid using timber which has an extremely uneven finish as it is likely to splinter with age.

Steps are only as sound as the base upon which they are built. While the measuring work necessary to ensure the steps are exactly the same height and width is relatively straightforward, the time-consuming part is the preparation of the slope. There is little point in creating a beautiful flight of steps in a garden if they are going to crack and become dangerous with the first instance of soil movement. To prepare the

foundation for the steps, all the unstable topsoil must be excavated or set aside. Bricks, paving slabs, slates, tiles, flat bush rocks or split stones should be set directly into a bed of mortar or concrete. Make sure they have been split along natural lines and not just sawn; this will mean they will weather better. Granite, on the other hand, must be sawn and polished professionally for the best results.

Construction will be easiest in a clay soil. After excavation you may find that only a sandy base or roadbase mixture is really required. Such a base is best suited to informal steps, such as

Things To Do

How about a rainbow garden? Nearly one hundred years ago a famous British gardener, Gertrude Jekyll, proposed this charming idea for budding young gardeners. Mark out some curved strips in a flower bed and plant red hot pokers, yellow marigolds, purple pansies, blue forget-me-nots, pink alyssum, and so on, which, when in bloom, will give you a beautiful rainbow in the garden.

rounds of hardwood, wide sleeper steps, or deep wooden blocks. Border shrubs can be placed to overlap and soften the edges, making for a very soft look. However, in sandy soils timber steps need to be attached to supports dug well into the ground or set in mortar. Usually a wooden frame in which to pour the mortar is also required. Use a spirit level to mark the horizontal treads on the vertical plank in the frame. This will help you to set up a 'profile' of where you want to build the steps and to accurately work out the height and width of each step.

Extra mortar may be used to fill in the spaces between the stones or tiles or, if it is an informal design, pack soil or sand in the cracks for eventual planting with sturdy groundcovers or herbs. Some of the prettiest small matting plants include thyme and mint; both give off a refreshing perfume when walked upon. You can also leave spaces beneath the steps, especially wooden ones, which can then be planted with shade-loving plants like ferns. Concrete can be used by itself to build steps, or in conjunction with other materials. Instead of being covered with bricks, slate or tiles, as above, concrete steps can be surfaced with pebbles or gravel to blend in more with a garden.

Another easy and environmentally sound way to build steps is to edge concrete slabs with old pieces of timber. Simply drill holes through the timbers and hammer reinforcing rods through the holes to hold them in position. This is a very popular choice in national parks and other areas that see a good deal of thoroughfare. Usually this type of step is finished with gravel or stone infilling for added hardiness. Remember, wherever possible, the timber pieces should be kept clear of soil and plants, thus reducing the risk that they will rot or become slippery and dangerous with lichens or moss. Stone steps can also become slippery when wet; ideally, they should be placed where they will catch several hours of bright sunlight each day to retard the growth of any fungi. They should also have a shallow channel cut into either side of their fall to discourage water from accumulating on the treads. Such a channel may be simply dug out and planted with low-growing, water-tolerant plants, or surfaced with concrete or tiles.

Verandahs and Decks

For a long time Australian houses have featured verandahs. They have served as a traditional meeting place between the house and its garden and have often been converted to provide extra sleeping accommodation in a growing family. Ideally, verandahs should be retained rather than closed in. They are an effective means of reducing heat and glare in summer and provide a shady, attractive area for children to play in year-round. From a design point of view, it is important that a verandah has reasonably generous proportions and should be at least wide enough to include a table and chairs where you can enjoy a cup of coffee. A verandah that is too narrow can act as an unnecessary barrier between the rooms of the house and the rest of the outside world.

In tropical far north Queensland, the verandah came into its own very early on. Broad, often spectacularly beautiful polished or painted timber verandahs were connected to the main part of older-style homesteads by tall French doors or louvred panels, and they often served as both a sitting room and a dining room. Typically, in more modest homes in areas of Australia where rain and high temperatures occur together, a curved corrugated iron roof was built out over the verandah as protection against a sudden downpour. The sound of summer rain on roofs like these — including the sudden hiss if the iron is hot from the sun — will often evoke memories in an expatriate Queenslander.

A well-designed verandah will provide an entertaining and recreation area for both adults and children

Honeysuckle (*Lonicera periclymenum*)

Blinds made from canvas, aluminium, bamboo, or wood can be used to create extra shade along the length of a verandah. Additional overhead louvres or pergolas, usually made from timber, give even more flexible shade control. Removable panels of metal, plastic, or wood are now available, and can be fitted into the sides or roof of a verandah; they ensure full shade in summer and can be taken out to let in the winter sunshine.

Shadecloth can be purchased in varying degrees of density and is a less expensive alternative for providing extra protection from sun, wind and fluctuating levels of moisture along an exposed verandah. Climbing plants can soften its appearance and effectively cut out excess heat or light. Shadecloth is particularly appropriate for ferneries or orchid collections and for other plants or shrubs that require a calm atmosphere and do not tolerate extremes of hot or cold.

Lush vegetation, such as ginger plants (*Hedychium*), jasmine, hoya vines and frangipani are all popular choices for growing alongside the edge of verandahs, often creating the sense of being in an enormous treehouse, surrounded by branches. In more practical terms, generous

Incorporating any existing trees when designing a deck adds interest to the structure

plantings around a verandah give extra protection from sun and glare, as well as filling the surrounding area with colour and scent, and helping to keep the atmosphere cool and moist. Thick underplanting with ferns such as stag's horn and elk's horn are most effective.

Many plants enjoy a verandah situation and the summer shade will reduce the need for watering. Even quite hardy plants, like ivy-leafed geraniums, star jasmine and grape vines will do best when they are sheltered from the hot westerly sun and relentless wind for which Sydney, in particular, is notorious. A pair of lemon trees in terracotta pots or figs (*Ficus hillii*) in painted Versailles planters also will do well when

Safety Tip

Do not use sticks for cooking on a barbecue or when camping — they may be poisonous. If you must use a stick, use a eucalyptus branch.

partially shaded from westerly sun and winds.

When deciding which plants you will place alongside a verandah, give some thought to how they will look with the sun shining through their leaves from behind. Jasmine and honeysuckle, for instance, tend to turn their faces towards the sun, providing only a view of twiggy undergrowth from the verandah, unless they are meticulously wired and trained. Star jasmine (*Trachelospermum jasminoides*), on the other hand, grows thickly and evenly to create 'walls' and even 'roofs' of cooling greenery and will look lovely viewed from beneath. It is a most endearing climber and flowers profusely in spring and summer and its glossy green leaves mean it still looks attractive for the rest of

A deck extends the living area of the house and bridges the gap between inside and outside

the year. I was sorry to have to cut ours down when we renovated the back of our house; happily, cuttings I took are now busily scrambling up and over the new brickwork.

The new growth of *Callistemons*, broad-leaved plants like *Hakea elliptica*, or even the obligingly easy-to-grow aluminium plant, also look wonderful when backlit by the sun's rays. Grape vines are probably one of the best choices for a delicious climber over and around a verandah. Not only do the ruby- and gold-coloured leaves look spectacular in autumn, but they provide bunches of wonderfully cooling, dusky-flavoured fruit in summer.

However, unless you are prepared to do battle with fungal diseases and attack by birds, stick to ornamental grape varieties. Wisteria is another possibility; its exquisitely scented drooping racemes of white, pink or purple flowers are very beautiful when viewed from beneath.

A deck is an elevated outdoor area, usually extending into the garden along the lines of an unroofed verandah. Whereas a verandah may be constructed from wooden boards, or paved or tiled, a deck is almost always made from wood. Also, like verandahs, decks are an ideal site for container plants or decorative pots and bowls filled with seasonal flowering plants. If the deck is reasonably sunny and safe from cats, you can make it a haven for birds by hanging a seed ball or bird feeder nearby and providing a bathing bowl or standard birdbath (see pages 166–7).

Decks are most appropriate for a sloping site; raised decks leading from a house on high foundations can greatly increase the amount of level, usable space available, and create an extensive outdoor living area. The best decks I have seen are built around existing trees, creating a truly magical 'Swiss Family Robinson' feeling of being in a treehouse. Ferns and other shade-loving plants may be planted beneath a deck to create a shady secret hideaway, either as a potential cubby-house, or for more prosaic purposes, such as shielding a toolshed or locking away pool equipment.

As with many other aspects of garden design, the important thing to remember when planning a deck is to allow for a generous measure of space. A deck that is too small can look rather mean and cramped and actually detract from any view, rather than blend pleasantly into the surroundings. Even if your deck does not have a marvellous view, judicious plantings around the perimeter can create a lively and interesting 'view'. Shade, provided either by new or existing trees or large market umbrellas, is a very important consideration. Not only must parents be ever-vigilant about the dangers of overexposure to the sun but, from a design point of view, a deck filled with unrelieved sunlight can lack interest and seem soulless. If the deck is not well-oriented and is overexposed to the sun, a pergola can be a wise investment (see pages 53–6), creating a comfortable compromise between light and shade and an opportunity to grow hardy sun-loving climbers like scarlet bougainvillea, or in colder areas climbing roses or wisteria which can change the whole look of this outdoor 'room'.

When planning a deck, be sure to select rough-sawn timber, especially if you are anticipating that it will be used frequently by children. Although there is the risk of splinters, the risk of slipping on a damp, smooth wooden surface is far greater. This consideration is even more important when designing a deck to create a level surface around an above-ground swimming pool. Slatted timber is the preferred material for this job, as it dries out more quickly. For safety's sake, railings or wooden balustrades around a deck must be solid. Continuous low seating around the edge of a deck is very attractive, allowing the eye an even flow to the view beyond. However, it will not safely double as fencing against inquisitive toddlers.

Wire mesh is probably the best choice for a family deck used by young children — it can easily be removed, for aesthetics' sake, when they are older. Also, ensure the deck is well lit, either from overhead or from low sources near the ground. The latter is probably preferable in the average suburban context as it will avoid light dazzling the neighbours!

Patios and Courtyards

Patios and courtyards are both extensions of the living area, creating a link between the house and garden. They enhance the overall garden design by introducing a creative use of space. A courtyard is usually a walled patio or terrace, with walls made from brick or concrete being erected to create a private suntrap and provide shelter from the wind.

In ancient Pompeii it was common for houses to be designed around a central courtyard or *xystus*. Courtyards were also popular in 17th-century Dutch and Flemish gardens and as a result, the design and manufacture of appropriately scaled stonework and sculpture became a craze. Urns, statues, pools and formal arbours decorated courtyard gardens belonging to the gentry while the high fences, built to give privacy from nearby houses, spawned a fashion for espaliered fruit trees. In slightly less law-abiding times, the courtyard was most often incorporated into formal country homes as an enclosed space where the household's food would be protected from bushrangers and thieves. The idea of a courtyard continued in Australia as an area where protection from extremes of climate could be achieved. Part-walled courtyards also featured as additions in large houses to provide space for cars and wagons.

Careful planning and design can maximise the potential of a courtyard garden

A courtyard should offer alternatives of sitting or playing in the sun or shade and protection from hot winds. The courtyard really comes into its own in the winter months. To make courtyards even more viable during inclement weather, a folding glass or perspex roof, which can be opened electronically, is worth saving for. A large protected courtyard, close to the living or family areas of the house, becomes a natural extension of the house and an ideal spot for casual or even formal outdoor dining. A courtyard sited near a swimming pool helps to give swimmers protection from the wind and becomes a suntrap, creating an idyllic environment in which to swim or loll in the sunshine. The walls can also be planned as a

safety measure for the pool surrounds.

If you do not like the look of bare walls, the luxuriant growth of thickly planted fast-growing ivies will quickly mask them. To prevent courtyard walls from becoming too sombre or 'closed-in', use variegated ivies, like *Hedera helix* 'Goldheart', which has leaves that glow like little jewels.

For both patios and courtyards there should always be a firm level surface large enough for a table and chairs for dining, as well as a chair or seat just for simple contemplation, and, if children are likely to be using the area a lot, there must be sufficient space for trundling a tricycle, spreading out toys and setting up an easel for drawing.

In small city gardens, the entire level area

may be paved to form a large patio which will serve as an outdoor 'living room'. In larger garden areas, a patio or terrace can be situated to create an interesting change of level or can be used to link different parts of a house, for example, a family room with a gazebo, poolhouse or granny flat. In a warm climate, paved garden areas scaled down to the proportions of large rooms become just that — another room of the house that can be used for much of the year.

In the family garden, a patio is the ideal spot for sunny outdoor entertaining and children's parties. Patios should be close to the kitchen and lounge or family room. Before siting a patio, ensure the area is large enough for your needs. If it is only large enough for one or two chairs, perhaps you could rethink it as a possible parents' retreat. If the patio is to be used by children, there must be room for some movement.

Shade, shape and materials are the other considerations for a patio. A pergola may be easily erected over a patio that has too much sun

(see pages 53–6). Climbing plants such as *Clematis microphylla* or *Cassia retusa* will tolerate even a very hot and dry aspect, providing some welcome shade and privacy for quiet play. Birds will be attracted to the climber *Agapetes meiniana* or you may plan for scent as well as shade with one of the jasmines, such as *Jasminum lineare* or *J. suavissimum*. Climbers that bear exotic blooms, such as the passionfruit (*Passiflora* spp.) or the hardier trumpet vine (*Campsis radicans*) suit warmer climates very well. Other good 'wall' plants, often used like climbers, are the beautiful evergreen *Ceanothus* species, or California lilacs.

An interesting shape can turn a patio into a really special spot. Do not settle for just a rectangular strip; consider curves or other irregular shapes as they tend to look far more attractive and create the illusion of space. An L-shaped patio, for instance, can be sited so that part of the patio is a very private nook, suitable for quiet reverie, and the rest faces the garden, pool, or adjoins the house itself. A narrow angled extension from a patio could lead to a path or

A sheltered courtyard provides an extra 'room' for entertaining

seat, or accent an interesting sculpture. Curved, fluid, interlocking shapes can be introduced to a rectangular patio or courtyard via a central series of flower beds. Are there any existing trees or shrubs in the area where you are planning to put your patio? Patios can easily run around a lovely old tree, which can then have a seat built around its trunk, creating an inviting place to sit. Even if there is no existing feature, it is easy to create one by installing a shallow pond or fountain (see

pages 66–71). One of the prettiest courtyards I have ever seen was set aside from the rest of the main garden. It had a tiny pool as a focal point with a potted orange tree in each corner and a luscious white wisteria clambering over the walls.

Low to medium stands of different shrubs can help create different effects around a patio. Planting creepers and sturdy groundcovers, like *Ajuga australia*, *Kunzea pomifera* and *Teucrium racemosum*, will quickly soften the break between the patio floor and the surrounding lawn or garden beds. Scented groundcovers, like *Mentha diemenica*, release their delicious scent when brushed against or walked upon, adding another pleasurable aspect to your patio.

Whatever material or pattern of laying you choose for your patio, the vital point is to take the time to put it down properly! Hurriedly laid pavers and secondhand bricks will soon buckle and crack, making the patio unsafe. An attractive patio is actually one of the easiest outdoor construction projects you will tackle. Cement slabs, crazy paving and cobblestones all require a reasonable level of experience, but laying bricks in a bed of sand is still the easiest and least expensive method of all. The most important trick to remember lies in proper preparation. The ground must be thoroughly tamped down to prevent hollows forming and the whole area should be gently sloped away to the garden to allow for adequate drainage.

When trying to work out the area of a complicated shape — for instance, a curved patio, or one which works its way around trees or shrubs — it is best to draw everything to scale on graph paper. Also remember there is no rule that states that the whole area must be paved. Leaving gaps between loosely laid flagstones or pavers, for instance, can create interesting detail if you plant in between the pavers. Nor should patio paving finish with a strongly defined edge, unless it flows straight onto steps. A staggered edge will merge more gracefully and informally into the garden, rather than separate you from it.

For small gardens, simple patio patterns and small pavers or bricks are most appropriate. One of the most effective techniques for making a patio or other paved area seem much larger is to lay the paving in curved patterns or in a series of circles. Herringbone, basket, or other linear patterns look good in rectangular or L-shaped patios. Clever angling of the bricks or pavers can

Paving with bricks, pavers or decorative floor tiles is a good option for a courtyard

even help lead the eye off to a sweeping view. Railway sleepers or seasoned wooden planks can be used for patios, provided they have a very sunny aspect. If wood is used in full shade, it can become slippery and needs to be regularly treated with mould retardants. Similarly, slate can become like glass when wet, so it is not a wise choice for a family patio. Pebbles, especially white ones, are a pretty and practical choice for a slightly shady courtyard, as they will assist drainage as well as being to an appropriate small scale (not such a good idea if you have a toddler who puts everything in his or her mouth, though).

My favourite patio flooring material is Sydney sandstone. It retains the warmth of the sun, making it ideal for basking cats, as well as adults, and the soft honeyed tones make for an aesthetic bonus. It will, however, stain easily; both red wine and oil will leave a permanent mark. A wide variety of mellow colours is available, whether you choose a natural stone or a commercially produced paver. Go for a medium tone — very dark stone can become unbearably hot for bare feet during summer and a very light-coloured stone or concrete can be unpleasantly glaring. From a design point of view, the flooring material should complement that used in the house. The walls of the courtyard should also echo the walls of the house proper.

As has been suggested, there are advantages in leaving pockets for growing shrubs or climbers to soften the impact of the surrounding house walls. In addition, patios and courtyards are ideal spaces for the gardener to enjoy container plants, which can be changed according to the season. In fact, plenty of paving and a wide selection of container plants is a terrific recipe for a garden that requires minimum maintenance. It is also an opportunity to indulge in slightly more temperamental plants, such as orchids or ferns, which prefer a warm protected area. Palms, figs, and lilies all look magnificent when planted out in containers. Of course, where winters are cold, these tubbed plants must be brought into a greenhouse or a cool but frost-free room.

It is also amusing to amass a collection of plant oddities. Children love to look at and touch the bright green cushion plant (*Scleranthus biflorus*) and, like most heathland or alpine species, it does well in a wide terracotta bowl, as do chubby little houseleeks or *Brachycomes*. The pots and tubs themselves can constitute an interesting and eyecatching collection, from tin cans to pots decorated with folk art, from magnificent Chinese enamelled tubs to oddments of old china. Let your imagination and personal preference dictate your choice.

Potted indoor plants may be brought out to the patio or courtyard for regular airings and

display. Before choosing plants which will be permanently sited on the patio, consider how they will fare year-round. What will be the effects of the weather — or of children? Do not plant ornamental chillies or prickly bougainvillea in such a spot (I speak from experience when I say that neither mixes well with children!). Evergreen shrubs, like *Murrayas* or New Zealand Christmas bush, are sturdy and attractive at close range year-round. Ferns may be moved into shadier areas during the heat of summer. They are also well suited to hanging baskets in shaded areas. When cultivating container plants, attention to good quality potting mix, regular watering, and drainage are all critical.

Tip

Encourage an awareness of the importance of recycling in children's minds from an early age. Glass jars, plastic margarine and ice cream containers, egg cartons and old plastic drink bottles may all be used for raising plants from seed.

Pathways and Paving

Pathways are an essential component of an informal, family-oriented garden. They enable people to walk on a secure surface and, during wet weather, one which is as dry and comfortable as possible. Pathways also provide practical access to service areas, such as clotheslines, compost heaps and greenhouses. Paths to service areas need only be quite small — long circuitous routes which disappoint by leading to a laundry can be avoided by siting the service area near the house and creating an attractive screen around it. This position will not ruin the view down the garden and will allow other paths to invite exploration of other more interesting parts of the garden.

A long vista framed in a series of gracefully adorned arches is probably impractical in a family garden. However, paths can still be used to great effect here to lead the eye around the area and intensify the effect of space. A path which leads to a focal point, such as a statue or pond, towards the front of the garden will draw attention to that area and, through the visual trick of foreshortening, will create a greater sense of depth beyond.

To assess what sort of pathways your garden requires, take the time to observe the soil and contour of the garden and the degree of sun and shade. These will affect the design of the pathway and how the surrounding area will be viewed. For instance, if the garden is shady and small, a pathway could be planned as quite dark and narrow, suddenly opening out onto a sunny lawn, which can actually increase the sense of depth. In a garden with wide sweeping lawns, curving paths alongside flower beds can enhance

the sense of space rather than running paths across the middle of the lawn, which will divide the area and look awkward. An obscured path brings a lovely sense of mystery to a garden. Children in particular love 'secret paths' through a garden and, by siting different plants to create screens and covers and, where possible, letting the edges become overgrown, you can turn a simple path into a journey of exploration.

An atmosphere of secrecy is most readily achieved with planting, but the shape and type of material used to surface the path will also be important. Bricks laid sideways, for instance, can make a path seem shorter; set lengthways they seem to increase the length of even a tiny path. The size of paving will also influence the speed at which people move over a pathway. Large stepping stones, for instance, are swiftly leaped over, while pebbles, stones and bricks can be used to make informal paths which encourage dawdling. Large stepping stones and raised wooden rounds are a more appropriate choice for an area that is sometimes wet or boggy, provided they are treated with an antimould solution to repel mosses and slime. Small shrubs and tufting plants, like *Correa decumbens, Stellaria pungens* or *Mentha diemenica,* are all suitable as cool climate groundcovers and would look pretty planted in the spaces in between the stepping stones.

If the path extends directly from a terrace it is best constructed from the same material as that used for the terrace to ensure a feeling of continuity into the garden. To soften the effect, a paved path leading away from a terrace can be surrounded by gravel, timber rounds or bark chips; plants and rocks overlapping onto a straight path will give the illusion of gentle curves.

Paths that are subject to frequent use or those that are used for transport should be hard-surfaced. A good rule is to make paths in all those places where the lawn has been worn bare by constant foot traffic. The choice of material is usually dictated by local geology and it is wisest — and cheapest — to stick with local materials. Imports, like marble, never seem to blend satisfactorily into an informal, family-oriented

A wooden pathway of old railway sleepers edged with creeping plants

garden. Paving slabs, bricks, stones or very well seasoned timber, on the other hand, are all suitable.

Old bricks and weathered stone make wonderful paths and even in a brand new garden they will soon look as though they have been there for years: such paths are best complemented by pleasingly disordered beds of mixed flowers and shrubs. If the path is wide enough, it is a pretty idea to leave gaps for specimen shrubs or for prostrate plants like thyme or creeping mint that will tolerate some foot traffic.

Bricks can be laid in many different patterns, though preferably on their edge in a herringbone formation. Care should be taken to select frost-proof bricks that will not split if water penetrates a crack and then freezes. For this reason old bricks are not always worth the trouble, no matter how appealing their patina or age may be.

*Be imaginative and create your own patterns
when laying pavers*

Flat stones make an attractive and stable path surface. Flagstones, sawn bluestone, sandstone, slate and bluestone pitchers are available in a wide variety of colours and may be chosen to complement the colours used in the house. If you are purchasing unsawn stone, be sure one face of each flag is smooth enough to walk on safely.

Stones of unequal size are best laid with the larger ones to the outside of the path, giving it stability. A brick edging to a flagstone path can also be very effective; similarly, reconstituted stone or concrete pavers can be made visually interesting. One example is to intersect slabs with lines of thick terracotta pavers or thin pieces of wood, or even decorative handmade tiles, if the budget allows. Otherwise, take inspiration from one of the most original approaches to decorative paving I have seen: 'stones' of different shapes and sizes were made by pouring concrete into a variety of old plastic containers — ice cream tubs, margarine

containers, yoghurt cartons — to a consistent depth of 6 centimetres. The whole family joined in the project and had a lot of fun preparing these whimsical and practical stones.

For highly used routes, pine bark chips, sawdust, gravel, or crushed quartz are all suitable. Even some grasses can be used as a path surface. Matting plants and some scented grasses, such as *Eragrostis brownii*, can turn a simple path into an enchanted spot. Children love grassy surfaces and such paths to create a special secret mood, allowing for the sounds of birdsong and rustling leaves as footsteps are muffled. Other examples of unusual and attractive grasses which may be used underfoot are silvery blue *Festuca glauca* and the tiny, iris-like *Sisyrinchium angustifolium*. *Holcus mellis* 'Variegatus' with pretty grey-green and cream foliage, makes a delightful surface for a path in dappled sunlight.

If the area for the path is shady, gravel and grass are the more appropriate choices; pavers tend to become slippery. However, gravel is not recommended for paths that slope, as the surface can be washed away in a heavy storm. An alternative is to mix the gravel or crushed material with concrete for extra stability. Natural pathways of crushed materials look very appealing but may not be suitable for an area of heavy foot traffic or near the house — for one thing, children's running shoes tend to pick up pieces of gravel or stone and they are endlessly tracked into the house. Similarly, I do not really consider earthen paths to be a good idea in the family garden, particularly if soil drainage is not perfect. Either way, soil or mud will be continually tracked indoors on shoes and pets' paws.

Crazy paving, where irregularly shaped and/or coloured pavers are assembled in an imaginative style, is a fun choice, especially if large, irregular pieces of stone are available, provided the area is not too damp. Very fine rock chippings or coarse sands make a good general cover for less-used paths. These sands are often available in interesting shades of red or ochre or grey, making them a potentially very imaginative choice. Pathways for even quite heavy use should be no thicker than 7.5 centimetres. They seldom need to be reinforced, though a light mesh is usually set down before laying a concrete path, especially a large one. A base under paths may not really be required in the case of gravel, chips or pebbles, however, for bricks, pavers or concrete, sand is relatively inexpensive and it is a good idea to use extra sand to build up levels for the path.

Bricks or pavers laid on a sandy base or an overly sandy soil should have a wooden edging to reduce movement. This is imperative for even gentle slopes if the soil is sandy because bricks can be laid directly into the earth. First excavate to the depth of the bricks and then level the soil so they lie flush with the adjacent surface. With any brick path, it is a good idea to keep away from the bases of trees as the roots

This pathway of irregular cut stone invites you to wander through the garden

will disturb the paving, making for an uneven and dangerous surface. Plastic or plastic mesh under gravel or pebble paths will retard weed growth. Plastic mesh has the advantage of allowing free drainage.

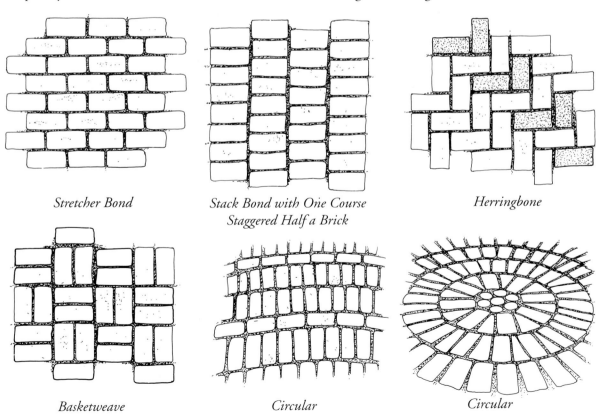

Stretcher Bond

Stack Bond with One Course Staggered Half a Brick

Herringbone

Basketweave

Circular

Circular

*A pergola over a pathway can create
a focal point in the garden*

small, you can make them look wider by arranging extra pavers, gravel, sand, or wooden discs along the sides. This will not only soften any severe lines but will allow for children sprawling sideways if they suddenly trip while running.

A winding pathway is more interesting and natural looking than a straight one, though a straight path may be suited to a formal front garden. The family garden tends to favour curving, generous paths with an indistinct edging. Before constructing your path, some thought should be given to the angle at which it will slope, so that water will drain away easily after it has rained. Ideally, paths should be laid with a slight camber towards a lawn or garden bed so the plants benefit from any run-off.

A popular addition to a path is the pergola, thus creating a shaded, colourful and sometimes scented walkway. Again, this is a valuable design trick to remember for a small to average-sized garden that everybody wishes to use for different purposes. A shaded path or walkway creates a focal point and a spot to dawdle, thus reducing the feeling of restricted space. Pergolas are easily assembled from sawn treated timber or may be purchased in kit form. The ever-popular planting choice for a pergola is to festoon it with climbing roses which fill the air with colour and scent during summer. A thornless variety, such as a *Banksia* rose, is the best choice if children are likely to be playing beneath. Beds filled with lavender, primulas, lilies, ferns and poppies set on either side can create a feeling of luxuriance in even a small space and act as a magnet for children in search of a shady, airy space to play.

If paths are in constant use they should be at least 1.3 metres wide. This is the minimum width that allows two people to walk alongside each other with relative ease. It also gives room for wheelbarrows and clothes baskets and allows plants to grow over the edges a little. It is silly having paths that force people to snake through the garden in single file. The only exception being if the paths are laid in a food garden where good use has to be made of limited space. Small narrow paths here mean that vegetables and salad crops may be planted more closely than in open ground. If you are planning your family garden around existing features in an established garden that includes paths which are too

Things to Do

Children love to smell flowers. Three old favourites that are most obliging in this regard are mignonette, bergamot and lavender. Show children how to brew bergamot leaves to make a herbal tea and to scatter dried lavender in the linen press to make sheets and towels smell nice.

Gates and Driveways

Gates are used so often that we tend not to think about them. However, with a little thought, they can be charming features in their own right. A gate should set the mood for the garden it opens onto and should be as attractive and secure as possible. Even a nondescript gateway can be made quite alluring by installing a rustic wooden arch or a simple trelliswork pergola supporting a pretty climber, like a Virginia creeper (*Parthenocissus quinquefolia*). In my neighbourhood a quite ordinary gateway has been turned into an appealing green 'porch' — two planter boxes have been set into the sides of the brick supports for the driveway gates and planted with box (*Buxus* spp.), which will eventually be clipped. A small ironwork arch has been set into the tops of the supports and this will be smothered with climbers in a season or two. This lovely gateway is not only a secure barrier between the house and the outside world, it is also an appealing garden feature and helps to create vertical interest to the fence line. If you are considering a climber-clad pergola or arch as part of a gateway, it should be designed to suit the house style and be in proportion to its distance from the house.

From a design point of view, a gateway should be well-defined. It is the transfer point between two separate places. The important points to remember about gateways are, firstly, that the gates should be complemented by wooden or masonry supports appropriate to their size, quality, and appearance; secondly, that they should go with the style and period of the house; and finally, that they are of a size and shape which will allow them to fulfil a function, either as a pedestrian walkway or to allow car access. For the former, an ideal width will be between 90 and 120 centimetres; for the latter, at least 2.4 to 3 metres should be allowed. (How many people, I wonder, have cursed the originator of a driveway gate as they have scraped the sides of their car?)

Gates provide security against uninvited people or neighbourhood dogs. Importantly, they keep children *in*. Regardless of the style of gate or the material you choose, promise yourself a sturdy childproof latch and, if you feel it is warranted, a padlock, at least while the children are small. Consider also the height of the gate relative to the surrounding fence. Gates about 90 centimetres high will keep most dogs out, but are easily scaled by even quite small children. If keeping inmates safe is your priority, gates should be at least 1.2 to 1.5 metres high. And, if security really does present a risk in your neighbourhood, a high gate with a small viewing hole is probably a wise idea. Very often the whole look of a house can be spoiled by unattractive or inappropriate gates and fences. If they are integrated into the fence, gateways will become part of a simple, unobtrusive boundary

that will not interrupt the flow of planting in any garden. The use of a muted paint will help unify this boundary, a trick worth remembering in very small gardens.

Wrought-iron gates come in all shapes and sizes and tend to work with most architectural styles. The 'see-through' look such gates provides can create an inviting sense of depth, yet still establish a safe boundary for pets and children. Many manufacturers provide a wide variety of gate styles, some mimicking Victorian cast-iron lace and others that may be powder-coated in green, white, bronze or black to complement the colours of the house.

Gates made from thick, broad planks which have been stained and then allowed to weather and soften slightly are a favourite look of mine. They always seem more welcoming than a freshly painted wooden gate. The colour chosen is a very important design element. My grandmother painted her front gate bright red and, even

though it was high enough to keep children in, it was still cheery to passersby. Similarly, yellow gates gleam attractively in a stone or brick fence while grey-green or brown gates are usually chosen to blend in more with surroundings.

If a rustic look would be more in keeping with your house, consider gates made from brush or even timber split into half-rounds. In old-fashioned gardens, such gateways were actually designed in such a way that they were concealed from passersby by overlapping the outer fence edges at a parallel in front of the gateway, creating an appealing mood of secrecy as well as increasing the feeling of security from the outside world.

Many other pretty styles and shapes present possible choices. Some residential styles really only look 'right' with an exact type of gate, for instance, the Spanish Mission style of house suits an over-the-top gate reminiscent of the gate in the Alamo fort, of film fame. Picket fences and

A stained wooden gate and brush fence screen this garden

Left: A grand wrought-iron gate at the entrance to a formal garden gives a hint as to what is inside

A charming white picket fence and gateway is the perfect entrance to a cottage garden

picket gates are usually a safe choice for a cottage while decorative wrought-iron gates go well with the classic stone or stucco fences of Georgian-style townhouses or terraces. A design of heavy piers and a pair of elaborate iron gates could be just the thing for a large imposing home. Or, for something completely different, what about a rounded or arched opening, or even the full circles seen in Chinese gardens? This could be lovely as the entrance gateway to a small town garden and would help enhance the feeling of a private oasis within.

Different materials will create different moods and effects. Wooden gates are usually manufactured from western red cedar or treated pine. In the interests of durability, a timber gate should always be combined with, or built onto, a steel frame to prevent warping. Similarly, old wooden or even leather strap hinges may have their place but not, in my opinion, in the family garden; anything other than strong steel hinges are going to be a nuisance.

Other gate furniture, namely handles, latches, and locks, should be selected for weather-corrosion resistance as much as for aesthetic and safety reasons.

Just as the gateway to a garden is like an entrance foyer in a theatre, so should the drive complement the garden. All too often we see suburban houses with short, straight driveways which do nothing to add interest to the home. Nor are they necessarily an optimum use of space, in fact, a loop driveway invariably provides better access, especially in a wide-fronted property. One solution to the narrow, awkward strips on either side of neighbouring driveways is to cooperate with your neighbour and, instead of a dividing fence, plant shrubs to form a thick screen between both driveways.

Practicality plays the main part in the design of a driveway. Thought must be given to the question of parking cars — and not just your own, either. What if friends drop by? Of course, such dilemmas are not always a concern

Safety Tip

Make regular checks on the safety of any swings, slippery dips or climbing frames in your family's garden.

in the small city property although it is here, more so than in a larger one, that the family driveway really comes into its own. It doubles as an open space for children to play in, unless of course it is so steep as to be dangerous, in which case you will need to ensure access is restricted with a side gate or childproof fence.

As with paths, care must be taken to lay the driveway so that rainwater does not collect on it. Commonly, runnels are placed on either side, which slope downwards to a central drain or grated pit, or the entire driveway may be graded down towards side gutters.

Surface materials suitable for driveways include brick pavers, cobblestones, gravel, asphalt, bitumen, wood blocks and concrete or concrete pavers. If, for instance, your driveway sweeps up and around a steep site, gravel would be a disastrous choice, and would probably wash to the bottom of the garden in the first heavy storm. Gravel is the traditional choice where there is a large area of level ground. If you are fortunate enough to have a large sweeping arc of a driveway leading up to your house, you will find the colour will harmonise better with the garden. Weeds are the scourge of gravel paths. Also, it is recommended that drains be built under or alongside gravel paths or driveways to carry away excess water.

Paving is a popular though more expensive solution for surfacing a driveway. It is also necessary on steep or exposed sites where it is important to be able to reach the house quickly and safely during wet weather. Rough-hewn pavers are more appropriate than those with a gloss finish in this instance, as they are less prone to becoming slippery. Antimould preparations should be purchased and sprayed onto new pavers if they have not already been treated in this way. Brick paving provides an attractive and durable finish.

I like planting trees along the edges of a driveway, creating a welcoming 'tunnel' of shade on hot days. Rhododendrons, firs and eucalypts (lemon-scented gums, or *Eucalyptus citriodora*) are all worth considering, the former for a slightly cooler aspect and climate, perhaps. When

planning a driveway flanked by trees, be sure to space them in relation to their eventual size. Remember that trees tend to droop after rain so prune low-hanging branches so they do not slap at the car or at unwary pedestrians. If space and proportion permit, a striking effect can be created by planting a pair of contrasting trees beyond the gate alongside the driveway, thus drawing the eye along the driveway. Strong contrasts of light and shade will be created if reasonable spaces are present between the trunks; otherwise the effect will be more hedge-like. Low hedges of, for example, clipped rosemary, can give a relaxed and countrified air to even a very short driveway. Upright dense screening shrubs, such as the Australian mintbush (*Prostanthera nivea*) and grevilleas or boronias are all suitable and look attractive even if they have to be trimmed quite hard to accommodate a narrow driveway.

Paving is a popular choice for surfacing a driveway

With an extremely steep driveway, concrete is probably the only really safe and hard-wearing option. This look is not to everyone's taste but the appearance of concrete pavers can be softened by leaving a space in the middle for groundcover plants, such as *Ajuga reptans*; remember that a curving driveway will always look more natural and less aggressive to the eye. Interesting surface textures may be created in concrete by drawing a small broom across the surface in straight lines, or by making diagonal patterns, zigzags and wavy lines.

Greenhouses and Garden Sheds

F amily gardens, with the emphasis on play areas and activities, can still be stylish and practical. With a degree of planning, a typical suburban garden can incorporate a functional section for growing fruit, vegetables and herbs. Not only will home crops of tomatoes, cucumbers and even apples make a worthwhile contribution to the weekly menu, but growing food will provide hours of pleasure for a very modest outlay and a small amount of effort. It goes without saying that a sunny aspect is needed; also, a well-nourished soil will go a long way towards producing successful crops.

Ideally, the food-growing section should be situated at one end of the garden. It may be fully or partially walled off, either with honeycomb

brick walls or trellis panelling fixed to stout wooden posts. Trellis has the great advantage of providing immediate screening and wonderful high-standing support for climbing vines. Before committing to order the readymade trellis panels on offer, examine them very closely. Unlike the decorative lattice used as infills for verandahs and decking walls, trellis that is going to be used for climbing vegetables or espaliered fruit trees should be sufficiently strong to support them

and to resist strong winds. They should be fixed with galvanised screws and bolts, which will resist corrosion.

For optimum results from your food-growing section, consider including a greenhouse. Greenhouses come in a wide variety of shapes and sizes and their objective is to provide a stable environment for the propagation and growth of plants that would not otherwise survive in the normal climate. In elegant old European homes, greenhouses were often quite fantastic constructions. It was very fashionable to cultivate rare tropical and subtropical plants. The family garden is more likely to give priority to salad crops or other delicacies which may be in short supply and difficult to buy or just plain expensive. Consider cultivating some plants purely for pleasure, though, such as orchids or gardenias, which require a constant temperature and prefer humidity. They can be potted in portable containers and wheeled into the garden or the house for special occasions.

Some greenhouses are very elegant and verge on being mini-conservatories, meaning they do not necessarily have to be hidden away at the bottom of the garden. I have seen one very pretty garden which featured a hexagonal greenhouse with a pointed roof as its centrepiece and it was very appealing, just like a cool ice cube. However, in the family garden, where there are likely to be ball games and romping pets, it is best to site the green-house behind a wall or as part of an enclosed terrace. If your garden has a windy aspect, the walls will afford greater protection for the glass structure as well as for the produce.

You might consider purchasing a cold frame for the food-growing section, too. They are very useful for hardening off seedlings before they are planted out and they may also be planted with

This garden shed has been disguised by growing ivy over its roof and walls, allowing it to blend in with the rest of the garden

salad vegetables and tender lettuces in cooler climates. Again, cold frames do not always mix well with children, pets or balls, so should be situated in a safe, warm corner of the food-growing section.

There are many prefabricated greenhouses available, made from steel or aluminium and — preferably — hardened glass. Most are built with full or partial roofs, which are usually vented. The roof panels may be made from glass though it is more usual that just the wall panels are glass. The radiant heat from the sun which is absorbed into the greenhouse through the glass walls is usually a more constant and gentle heat than that which comes directly from overhead. Check what facilities your greenhouse model offers for regulating temperature. Most will have high-level vents for flushing out overheated air and drip or spray water systems are standard

accessories. Additional canvas roller or folding shades extending from the glass walls are worth considering in a warm climate, while a central stove or heater (often operating on hot water) is necessary in a very cold climate.

Fruit cages are another worthwhile idea. Unless fruit is protected with netting, birds and possums can ruin a crop overnight. A cage made from a wooden or steel tube frame and 'walled' with netting is a relatively simple project for the home building enthusiast. It is also an aesthetically pleasing alternative to tying plastic bags and other bird-scaring devices to the trees. A fruit cage may be converted to a shadehouse later on by changing the netting to shadecloth.

Brush and sapling shading is another possibility; this is more expensive than the black or green mesh, but provide a superior effect and denser shade. Shadehouses are

particularly suitable for ferns and other plants which like filtered sunlight. A pretty idea is to incorporate the shadehouse with a garden path so that passersby walk among the pots of plants. A shadehouse can also double up as a sheltered sitting area for adults and children. My neighbour has a long, angled shadehouse that follows the contours of his garage from east to west, thus maximising the available shade. A small, south-facing wing, where he transplants new seedlings, has recently been added. And the most attractive place to site a shadehouse is often beneath a large, spreading, shady tree, such as an oak or a eucalypt. Freestanding shadehouses are an ideal support for climbing roses, wisteria or ivy.

Every garden will require a shed for storing all the tools and accessories necessary for maintaining a garden. You will need an area that is at least 2 metres square for storing the wheelbarrow, mower, and tools, plus shelves for bottles and boxes and a lockable cupboard for poisons. A sturdy workbench down one side (preferably that lit by the window) is a must for potting seedlings and other grubby jobs.

Depending on the size of your food-growing section the shed should be sited close to it, as it makes for easier working. However, it is also important that the shed be a decent size — one that is too small will quickly become overcrowded, with items left outside, defeating the purpose of building the shed in the first place. If the food-growing area is too tiny, try to build the shed from materials that blend with the garden, such as treated pine, red cedar, or brown- or green-painted hardwood. Of course, there are many prefabricated aluminium sheds

Safety Tip

Minimise the amount of exposed skin when gardening, especially when pruning trees or shrubs which may have sap that can cause an allergic reaction. Always wear gloves and keep your arms covered. Apply a protective sunblock or sun cream, preferably with a Sun Protection Factor (SPF) of 12 or more.

available but these are often unattractive and some form of screening, either with a fence or with plants, will be necessary.

When siting your shed, try to place it so that it is not in the main view from the house and ensure that the ground is well-drained. A firm, level base is needed as ground movement will distort the frame. Some sheds are supplied with a sturdy base, but the majority require a concrete slab to be laid by the gardener. Alternatively, consider paving slabs or leftover concrete blocks as the base for the shed. A strip of damp-proof course or roofing feet should be placed around the base to further preserve the shed, particularly if you plan to smother it with plants.

Ensure the shed is well ventilated. Air circulation reduces the risk of vapours from chemicals (especially pool cleaners and antifungal preparations) becoming concentrated in the atmosphere if the shed is shut up for a time. When choosing a location for either a shed or a greenhouse, it is also convenient to have an electric light and at least one power outlet.

Place the door of the shed out of general view, as the contents are not always attractive when the door is left open. Nor are they likely to be safe if children are around. Install a high latch and secure it with a plastic-covered weatherproof bolt and padlock set available from hardware stores. Ensure any shed window is just as secure.

Finally, remember that many council authorities will require a permit to construct a garden shed or greenhouse, depending on its size and proximity to the boundaries of the land. It is usually worth checking local requirements before assembling the finished product.

Left: Garden sheds should be in keeping with the style of the garden

Soft, Sunny Lawns

My husband's eyes go all misty when he describes his ideal lawn — lush, smooth, bright green and immaculately kept. The appearance and easy maintenance of a lawn is important to both the overall look and the usefulness of the family garden. A smooth, well-kept lawn is a desirable focal point for a garden and, large or small, can be set down in varying shapes that can evoke different effects. It is also a perfect place to run races, skip, roll or just loll in the sun.

The shape and flow of your lawn is an important aspect of the garden's design. Do not attempt a lawn on a site that is just too small. Any bordering plants will look squashed and prim. The ideal lawn should create a feeling of space and generosity. In a garden to be used by all the family, first decide how much open space is required for games and races and then soften the borders by planting trees that will cast welcome shade on the players. I particularly like the look of lawns that have been shaped imaginatively around big sweeping flower beds heaped high with brightly coloured shrubs. Such an interplay between colours and textures creates interest in the garden, as well as creating the illusion of more space. Children are also more likely to prefer a lawn with contours and shadows to a boring backyard rectangle.

The groundwork for a lawn needs to be considered very thoroughly if it is to be a success. Before sowing a lawn, consider its aspect and

A beautifully manicured, healthy lawn is every gardener's dream

eventual use. Is the lawn likely to be subject to a great deal of foot traffic? If so, plan for a lawn which integrates planted and paved areas. Does much of the area fall in shade? Many grasses will not thrive under old or established trees, so consider planting sturdy groundcovers like *Ajuga reptans* or native violets instead. The latter are very dainty with their masses of blue and white flowers. Children love to pick little posies of tiny flowers like these in secret garden nooks and use them for doll parties and the like and the flowers are most obliging about growing back quickly.

Pratia pedunculata is a pretty and hardy groundcover with bright yellow flowers, which grows well in sun or shade, provided you keep up the water. Some herbal lawns, notably chamomile and thyme, are highly practical as well as fragrant and will often grow quite well where lawn grasses will fail due to lack of light or water. The best lawns, in my opinion, are the ones which are not entirely given over to growing grass alone. In spring, change your lawn's personality completely with a sweep of daffodils or clumps of bluebells, scillas or crocuses seeping out from beneath a tree.

Once you have decided where you would like your lawn you can start preparing the soil. Soil preparation should be carried out in late summer or at the end of winter. Clear all plants and existing vegetation, other than any shrubs you particularly want to keep as features. If you wish, now is the time to apply a selective weed killer to get rid of any deep-rooted weeds, such as the nefarious fishbone fern, which can ruin a new lawn. This step, however, is only for the purists — a strong, healthy, thickly planted new lawn should quickly choke out any weeds.

A clayey soil should be prepared with a rotary hoe and

Steps are often used to connect different levels in a garden

then gypsum should be worked through the soil. When preparing this base, be sure to allow some fall, even across a level lawn, to avoid boggy patches developing. The next step is to rake a friable, humus-based sandy loam through the surface, finishing up with an upper layer up to about 5 centimetres thick. Water the surface to identify any final dips or holes where water could accumulate, and then smooth them out. Finally — the fun part — sowing the seed or planting the turf. Some brands have slightly different instructions but the general idea is to rake the surface gently, scatter the seeds or lay the turf and then rake the soil over the top of the seeds, or roll the turf gently into place and water carefully.

Now that you have established your lawn, give some thought to the size and style of lawn mower you will require, unless you plan to budget for the cost of a gardener or contractor to do the job. Most modern rotary mowers will do a more than accurate job, provided any slopes in the garden are not too steep. Also, consider buying or building a garden shed (see page 47) if you do not have anywhere to store your mower.

Things to Do

If there is an old spare tyre in the garage, why not recycle it as a raised garden bed for the children? Place the tyre flat on the ground and fill it with soil, then plant it with bulbs, flowers and seedling vegetables such as carrots or herbs, which the children can tend.

2

OUTDOOR FEATURES

Lights and Safety

Garden lighting will create drama and atmosphere; it will also bring out the magical beauty of your garden by night. The family garden becomes a charming place for children and adults alike to while away a balmy summer's evening. Fragrance seems to linger on the air, the flowers' colours seem more intense and, with clever lighting, any garden defects become alluring plots of shadow which beckon children for a game of hide-and-seek after dinner.

Flickering outdoor candles can provide an appealing, if dim, glow and will produce a magical effect in a garden. Regrettably, candlelight is not really an option in the family garden for safety's sake. However, there is an enormous variety of garden lighting available, which will satisfy both practical and aesthetic considerations. Garden lighting need not be intrusive and may be planned to blend in well with your house and surroundings.

Lighting can illuminate favourite trees and shrubs or attractive features, such as statues or a pool. Sometimes, even flooding an area which is

nondescript by day with a green or red light can make it a surprising garden feature by night. On a more practical note, garden lighting will deter intruders and help avoid accidents on dark side paths or around entertaining areas or the pool.

Underwater lighting is a glamorous option for the pool owner, providing soft light and creating an interesting garden feature at the same time. Children will love being able to play and swim after dinner on a summer's evening, the lighting extending the time in which they can safely and enjoyably use the garden. Driveway lighting is also a must, for safety and security reasons.

Angling additional lighting near your barbecue area can give you an extra 'room' by night, a spot in which to eat that is not right next to the smoke. A good tip to remember when lighting the barbecue itself: use two lights, one from either side. Otherwise, the cook will always be working in his or her own shadow. Floodlights are probably the most practical choice here. Something else worth remembering is that

Left: Subtle, well-positioned lighting can create a pleasant atmosphere in a garden

*Lighting in the garden not only adds atmosphere,
it is an important safety consideration as well*

particular tree with fairy lights — an effect that will delight both children and romantically minded adults. Alternatively, underlight the tree, directing a soft light upwards. High pressure sodium lights will give a warmer look than the bluish glow typical of mercury lights.

Spotlights certainly provide good lighting, in fact, they can make the whole garden as bright as day! As they are not particularly subtle, spotlights are only recommended for areas where they are really needed, such as food preparation areas or steps. If they are to be fastened to eaves, take care that they are not angled directly at the garden as the effect can be blindingly unpleasant. Backlighting, low-height lights and even strings of mini-lights will give a high quality of light with minimum glare.

Whatever lighting system or mood you hope to achieve, it is important to seek specialist help as you will need a waterproof transformer and leads to be correctly installed. A specialist can also help provide a flexible system so that lights can be moved around or used in different combinations. With children around, it is important that the mechanics of your lighting system are well concealed: armoured cable should be buried at least 60 centimetres underground (check local regulations as there are some differences, depending on the area) and, ideally, they should be sited alongside a path for ease of access and retrieval. A lighting expert will be able to give advice on the number and location of switches and any other related devices, such as timers or security sensors. And, even though it is not a legal requirement, it is only common courtesy to ensure that your neighbours are not going to be disturbed by your lights.

amber or golden glass will reduce the number of insects attracted to the area. Mosquitoes and midges gravitate towards dark clothing, so dress the children in light-coloured skirts or shorts to minimise attacks.

There are two general ways to light outdoor areas: either from overhead or at ground level. Usually a combination of both will give the best results. Only low-wattage bulbs are necessary. A very pretty idea is to light the inside canopy of a

*Lighting should be unobtrusive
where possible*

Pergolas, Canopies and Awnings

Good dappled shade can be created by a simple pergola, whether built over an eating or drinking area adjacent to the family home, or situated elsewhere in the garden as a freestanding feature.

One or two climbers, such as grape vines, an ornamental vine like a Virginia creeper (*Parthenocissus quinquefolia*) or the aptly-named 'mile-a-minute', *Polygonum baldschuanicum* will quickly cover the bare structure. Certain trees, especially laburnums and some fruiting trees, also do very well when trained about a pergola. For best results, train the leader stems upwards and run the lateral stems horizontally; otherwise the whole lot will just race up and over the pergola, leaving the sides empty of foliage. When the leaders are meeting overhead, either twine them together and let them keep growing or — if you have planted a pair of identical plants — emulate the old vineyard practice of grafting them together, creating, in effect, a single plant with two root systems.

Seen from the underside, wisteria provides an interesting pattern, as does the more tender Chinese star jasmine (*Trachelospermum jasminoides*). A generously flowering and richly scented climber, star jasmine will provide a luxuriant roof of greenery that will help to keep a pergola cool in summer. The generally hardy clematis and honeysuckle and more tender passionflower (*Passiflora* spp.) are all attractive options when selecting climbers for a pergola. An old-fashioned rose can turn a pergola into a truly memorable garden feature. Good choices include the extraordinarily vigorous Himalayan musk rose (*Rosa brunonii*), *Rosa moyesii* with its lush scarlet flowers and *Rosa* 'Albertine', a

Clematis is a good choice when selecting a climber for a pergola

beautiful old-fashioned rambler with salmon-coloured blossoms. Especially pretty and unusual is the climbing hydrangea, *Hydrangea petiolaris*, though, as it clings by aerial roots or tendrils, some wiring or taping may be necessary.

The charm of a pergola increases as it becomes somewhat wildly overgrown with climbers and this process can be aided by clothing the whole structure with wire or plastic-bonded mesh. It may look a little rough to start with, but will quickly mellow under a canopy of entwined stems of climbers. Similarly, latticework or shadecloth can be added to the top of the pergola beams to hasten the development of a thicker roof.

Quite apart from the practical advantages of providing shade in the family garden, including shady plots and nooks will enhance the overall aesthetic appeal of the garden. Children love to play in and around a pergola, ducking first from the bright light into the scented shadow and

then out into the bright light again. Perhaps their play can be likened to the idea of surfacing from beneath water and then plunging under again. Pergolas create the feeling of a pleasing or secret enclosure which children, always on the lookout for fantasy and adventure, will love.

As a general rule, plan for about one square metre of shade for every sunny one. To do the job properly for the long-term enjoyment of all the family, contact the local Bureau of Meteorology and find out the angle of the sun at midday, both during midwinter and midsummer, before siting your pergola. Then, corner a friendly architect and ask him or her to plot where the shadows will fall.

Aim for an integrated balance between light and shade throughout the garden. For instance, you might plan to set up a pergola on the northern sunny side of the house rather than on the southern side which, likely to be shady already, will create a clammy and quite

depressing spot in winter. Of course, if sun is preferable in a pergola in winter time, it is a simple matter to plant only deciduous plants which, when their leaves drop, will let in a great deal of sun. A grape vine is probably the best choice for a deciduous climber. And, for sentiment's sake, opt for a fruiting variety rather than an ornamental one. From a child's point of view, it is a magical and memorable thing to be able to pick a bunch of sweet, sun-warmed fruit and eat it straight from the vine .

From a design point of view, a pergola should complement the house in terms of mass, weight and style. For instance, if your house is large and solid, the pergola should be too. With a smaller wooden cottage, a pergola of slender wooden or bamboo columns and equally slender crossbeams, perhaps finished off with some latticework or wood, or even wrought-iron in-fills, would look more appropriate. Other choices include swirled stucco, fluted cast iron, fluted timber or decorative stone (or fake stone) columns, which can be especially matched to a house's materials or style. Usually, square wooden beams (either oak, treated pine or stripped logs) will suit many family homes. The columns should either be secured in a base of dressed stone or brick, or be bolted to a galvanised steel foot which, in turn, is set well into the ground.

A good tip to remember is that the pergola should look as attractive unadorned as when, ultimately, it is covered with plants. Also important is to plan for pleasing proportions. The top should be set at least 2.1 metres above the walkway to avoid any sense of oppression and to allow climbing plants to hang down gracefully without slapping at an adult's face. Depending on the size and the type of plant you wish to grow over it, additional strengthening may be required in your pergola, particularly if it is a

Things to Do

Sprouting seeds is fun for everyone. Sprouts of alfalfa and mung beans are very nutritious and tasty in salads. They are easily grown in a jam jar on a warm window sill. The seeds start to shoot on the first day and the resulting sprouts can be eaten in less than a week. The seeds have to be rinsed two or three times a day, and this teaches children that plants have to be looked after on a regular basis.

While providing shelter, a pergola still gives the sense of being outdoors

Create a shaded, colourful and even scented area by growing climbing plants over a pergola

freestanding one. If the pergola is attached to the main building this is less of an issue, as the adjoining wall provides bracing.

Pergolas may also be made by arranging purchased metal arches in a row or an L-shape. This concept is especially attractive when used to link one part of the garden to another, creating a living, shady 'tunnel'. Often a pergola used this way can be a subtle way of playing a screening role and diverting the eye from the perimeter of the garden; in this case, an attractive seat or lovely plant will enhance the sense of sanctuary. Pergolas can create depth and

Tip

Encourage children to enjoy gathering seeds for sowing. Seeds can be collected from the garden when plants have developed ripe seeds, and it might be worth experimenting with seeds from fruits and vegetables brought home from the greengrocer's, such as pumpkin.

perspective, as well as a sense of mystery, within even a small family garden. Children in particular will be intrigued by a view of a mirror-backed vase at the end of a pergola.

An even more fanciful lure for a really imaginative garden would be a crystal orb, a device much used in 18th-century European walled gardens to play tricks with light and shade. If little fingers are likely to be patting a 'magic' vase or orb for luck, be sure it is firmly cemented to its pedestal. That way children and adults will both be able to enjoy the feature for years to come.

If you are still in pursuit of shade, awnings will cover doors and windows to protect you and your family from the harsh rays of the sun and will also protect the life of your furniture and curtains. Advanced roller shutters may be an option. These keep out the heat in summer and stop the cold coming in during winter. Most of these blinds will open and shut manually, although an increasing number now have electronically controlled systems. Some incorporate wooden or plastic slats or louvres which may either be adjusted to control the degree of summer sun received, or removed altogether during winter months to allow in maximum winter sunshine. Such overhead louvres are a little more expensive but are definitely worth the amount of money involved, particularly in a family-oriented garden where, ideally, all parts of the land can be used at all times of the year. More usually, awnings are made from colourful acrylic fabrics which will wear much better than the old-fashioned canvas ones.

Glass walls and full-length windows allow a garden to become part of your indoor living area but, whereas in winter the additional reflected warmth may be welcomed, in summer the amount of heat and sunlight will need to be reduced. Permanent features which provide summer shade, while allowing the winter sun to penetrate, include making the roof's eaves wider to the west and north, adding wide verandahs around the house or planting trees in positions which cast shade on different areas in summer and winter. Shadecloth awnings provide a removable or permanent shade option and effectively cut out up to 70 per cent of the heat and light, depending on the material's density. Such awnings are particularly suitable for the southern or eastern wall of a fence or house.

Depending on your requirements, it is worth investigating outdoor canopies made from sunscreening fabrics, reputed to cut out 85 per cent of the heat while continuing to let the light through. Some enterprising manufacturers have produced clothes hoist covers made from such fabrics. These provide a welcome and sizeable pool of shade for a family meal on a hot day, as well as being a quick, portable and inexpensive alternative to a permanent, plant-covered pergola. Also available are canvas clothesline covers or canopies and other models made from water-resistant polyethylene fabric. Remember that although 'sunscreen' fabrics will markedly reduce the impact of the sun's heat, they do not guarantee to actually screen out the harmful UVA and UVB rays. Between the hours of 11 and 3 in summertime, children, and indeed adults, should always wear a hat and apply a maximum protection sunblock to all exposed parts of their bodies when outside.

Practical Barbecues

What would the Australian backyard be without a barbecue?

A barbecue can be as simple or as sophisticated as you like. One of my fondest memories of my father is of him grilling chops and sausages every Sunday, 'to give your mother a break from the cooking'. Summer entertaining can be both stylish and easy, with a menu of barbecued chilli prawns and carpetbag steaks for

Lighting the area around your barbecue enables you to use it any time of the day

seats and the barbecue for standing space. Two tips to bear in mind when building a permanent barbecue: be sure to choose bricks or stones that will be least likely to be stained by dripping fat or smoke. Light coloured brick or concrete blocks would probably be a mistake. Secondly, try to choose a location that will allow for alternative working positions, according to wind direction. Ideally, you should not have to stand with your back to your guests while cooking. Similarly, children's play areas should be clearly visible from the barbecue area, particularly if the children are very young. For peace of mind, probably the best design for a permanent barbecue in the family garden would incorporate some sort of brick retaining wall, allowing access to only one person, the chef, on the side where the fire is being stoked. Be sure to incorporate a shelf for serving the food onto plates — and a corner to keep a well-earned glass of wine or beer handy!

If planning a permanent barbecue as part of a renovation to a new or existing pool or cabana area, you might consider getting professional advice about installing a chimney. However, you must be prepared to clean it regularly, or it will fail to draw properly and your guests will be engulfed in smoke. You should also consider either making or buying a weatherproof metal lid to fit over the grill area when the barbecue is not in use, to deter vermin. Alternatively, be sure

adults, plus sausages and hamburgers for the children. You can even do breakfast on the barbecue in summer — eggs, bacon and savoury pancakes taste delicious when cooked outdoors. Provided you observe some simple safety rules, barbecues are a boon to the family garden; children can run, eat and play and even spill food without causing any harm.

Just as everyone has his or her own favourite barbecue recipe, a barbecue itself is a very personal choice. A barbecue or charcoal grill can be a permanent structure made from bricks or stone. One advantage of a permanent barbecue area is that you can build in seats or storage space for fire-making materials. The simplest style to attempt is a brick structure with one or two grids cemented into place over the fire area and storage space at one or both ends. For the more ambitious, try planning a circular barbecue, centring the barbecue beneath a shady tree and arranging two semicircular seats around the barbecue and paving the area between the

Think carefully when designing a barbecue, ensuring sufficient room for cooking and serving food

to scour the area well. Some people use the barbecue grill as a shelf for pots of vermin-repelling herbs, such as tansy and spearmint, when it is not being used.

If the idea of a permanent barbecue does not appeal, there is an enormous variety of portable gas or electric barbecues now available. These can be a great deal more practical, and mean that cooking and eating can take place in different parts of the garden, depending on the time of day and year. The newer portable barbecues boast a fantastic range of options for the outdoor cooking enthusiast, from Japanese-style hot-coal grillers for char-grilling fish steaks, to covered broilers for steaming or stewing at the same time as barbecuing. Different-scented woods, such as hickory or juniper, eucalyptus, or even lavender, can be added to the barbecue wood to give food a wonderful aroma. Similarly, balsamic vinegar and apple cider vinegar can be splashed over hot coals when cooking seafood or chicken to enhance the flavour.

Swimming Pools

Private swimming pools are not a new idea. The remains of 5000-year-old tiled pools and courtyards are still visible in Asia, India and Egypt. Yet, never before have so many families considered integrating a pool into their lifestyle.

The warm climate of most mainland Australian cities means that Australians can spend much of their leisure time outdoors. A swimming pool, therefore, becomes a spot where you and your family can relax and entertain guests. It is also a healthy exercise centre in your own backyard and a playground for your children — perhaps even a training centre if they are aspiring swimming or diving champions! The cost of installation has become comparatively cheap and as, sadly, beaches have become more polluted and crowded, a private swimming pool makes good sense. Also, adding a swimming pool to your property will increase its total value.

The design and location of a swimming pool are of key importance for creating harmony between the pool and its surroundings. Put simply, it is best to opt for an aesthetically pleasing shape that is not highly specialised. A family pool is primarily used for relaxation and entertainment and a design combining a shallow area to splash around in, space around the pool for lounging and a nearby shaded area for tables

Things to Do

Children soon become curious about what happens when you plant a seed or pip from something they have eaten. Many of these will germinate successfully to form attractive houseplants. Oranges, lemons, dates, tomatoes, and even more exotic fruit like mangos, lychees, and avocados, will soon shoot if they are planted in a peat-based soil.

When landscaping a pool, take into consideration the style of your garden. This pool blends well with the natural setting of the garden around it

and chairs will provide the most useful prospect in the long term.

Nor is there any need to feel constrained by the normal, fairly small, rectangular suburban plot. Experiment with several pool-and-landscape schemes until you find one that suits your family's lifestyle and taste. For instance, a free-form pool lends an informal touch, which can be carried through by planting groups of graceful trees and shrubs. A geometric-shaped pool can produce a strikingly different effect, complemented perhaps by a raised, paved area for a barbecue. A rectangular pool is easily positioned down the sunniest side of the block of land — where it can possibly take advantage of any view — while fencing on the opposite side can be built up to shield swimmers from the view of neighbours.

You can play tricks on the eye by using colour and perspective with your pool. For instance, a dark-surfaced swimming pool will harmonise well with natural surroundings and will appear to take up less room in a small backyard than a more brightly coloured one. A dark-bottomed pool will also attract slightly more solar heating if it is located in full sun. Pool contractors today can undertake to paint the pool in just about any colour you choose — a pale green can be very pretty, while a greyish marbled effect (or real Italian Carrera marble, if price is not a problem!) reflects the colour of the sky on any particular day. Think about installing underwater lamps (see page 51), especially if your family entertains a good deal. The glowing, softly suffused light can create a magical effect for a pool party.

If the ruins of ancient Roman pools are anything to go by, choosing a pool site is a most important decision and certainly one you will have to live with for a long time. The main practical considerations when siting a pool are that it should have maximum exposure to the sun and protection from the wind, thus making for a pleasant environment in which to swim or sun yourself. (Also, the person who is most likely to be responsible for cleaning the pool should ensure it is sited as far away as possible from any trees that shed their leaves!). With a new house, the swimming pool and its surrounds can be planned at the same time, making for a well-integrated design.

However, it is more usual to install a swimming pool as an improvement to an existing house and property. In this instance, be sure to study your property thoroughly and familiarise yourself with its features and climate; try to evaluate several possible pool sites. Remember, it is the weather and aspect that will determine how comfortable your pool and the surrounding area will be. Watch to see how the sun travels across your garden and where, if at all, it lingers the longest. A pool that faces north is bound to be warmer year-round than one with a southern exposure. Too much wind blowing across a pool can rob it of heat, as well as send shivers up the spines of wet swimmers. Try to place your pool where it will make maximum use of the available sunlight during summer hours and where it will be most protected from wind. By effectively positioning the pool to take maximum advantage of the sun and protecting it from the wind, you will have taken the first steps to reducing the costs of heating your pool water, too. If the budget allows, consider installing a solar water heating system so your family can swim year-round. Similarly, invest in a pool cover; this will help to trap heat as well as keep out insects and debris.

If there are no natural windscreens present (for example, rocks and trees), create a sun trap with fences, screens or trees. A courtyard, by virtue of being an enclosed space, has a great practical advantage for a swimming pool, giving both protection from the wind and acting as a

Walls, fences or screens can protect a pool area from wind and create a sun trap

*Whether the fence is decorative or purely practical, all swimming pools should be fenced
as a safety precaution*

sun trap, plus helping to contain any noise, especially from children! The walls are also ideal supports for pretty, flowering, climbing plants — roses, honeysuckle and jasmine are all favourites around a swimming pool — contributing colour and fragrance to the general atmosphere of fun and pleasure.

Practical considerations to keep in mind when selecting your pool site include:

• The paved area. Ensure that the materials used are of sufficiently rough texture that they provide a non-slip surface without being too harsh on small bare feet. Also, think about the amount of space you need in the paved area. Ensure there is plenty of room for sunbathers and enough run-back for people wanting to dive into the pool. Flagstones are a very attractive choice, though an expensive one. Bricks can be picked to coordinate with the brickwork used for garden beds or in the house itself; the newer interlocking concrete blocks provide a visually pleasing and practical alternative. Artfully arranged decking is a useful screen for above-ground pools and can be shaped around favourite trees.

One rule of thumb states that the area for poolside activities should be at least equal to the area of the pool itself, in order to be proportionate from a design point of view, as well as providing a reasonable amount of space for people to sit, lounge, and sunbathe. Each person will require, for comfort, an area of about 0.9 x 1.8 metres, plus a decent gap between each person.

• Location of trees, shrubs and lawn. Planting should ideally be devised to create a visually pleasing blend of light and shade and to complement the bright, sparkling water. I would recommend planting large trees well away from the swimming pool, thus reducing the risk that their roots will disturb the pool's foundations and lessening the likelihood of leaves dropping in the water. Choose a tree with its eventual height and shape in mind; ideally the sun, as it passes overhead, should throw a continuous shadow from your tree(s) onto the area where a

table and chairs have been set up, so that the family will always have the option of sitting in some cooling shade during the heat of the day.

Lawns should be kept well away from the edgings around the pool, or else lawn clippings will end up in the water whenever the grass is mown. Gazanias are extremely practical for poolside use. Not only are they bright and colourful, but they love full sun and are hardy enough to take regular splashings of pool water, or even being trampled by little wet feet.

• Consider access for all the heavy earthmoving equipment that your pool contractor will be using.

• Do not plan to site the pool anywhere that will interfere with easements. There must always be access for services such as gas, electricity and water.

• For the family with small children, the pool should be sited where it is easily and pleasantly viewed from the kitchen and/or family room in the house.

• Give some thought to future landscaping requirements before you site your pool; in particular, anticipate any privacy problems you may face from your neighbours. For instance, even though you may have thought of using fences, trees and shrubs to help you screen your pool at ground level, will your neighbours have a bird's-eye view of your activities from their second-storey window?

Landscape artists will generally advise that swimming pools are best sited well away from the house and the main body of the garden. Unless very well planned, with a clever linking device such as a paved area, a swimming pool can be displeasing to the eye if it seems to butt up against the back door. If you feel you could do with some professional help when planning your pool, collect recommendations of pool contractors from other pool owners; alternatively, look in the telephone book and contact several nearby contractors for an obligation-free opinion. It pays to be very thorough in the initial stages of planning your

All swimming pool fences and gates must be childproof

councils require every pool to be surrounded by a childproof fence 1.2 metres high with self-closing gates. Be sure to consult both your local council and the health and building departments to find out what restrictions, codes and other regulations will apply to your garden. When you have this information, investigate the wide variety of fences and screens available and decide which is most suitable for your family. For instance, steel or wrought-iron fences safely close off a pool from other play areas but keep it highly visible. If the pool takes up most of the garden, you might like to consider decorative brick walls or wooden stockade style fences which complement the pool and its surrounds.

A HOP, SKIP AND A SPLASH

A pool can transform your backyard into a recreation and entertainment centre. Here are some ideas for family fun and fitness:

• One option is to install a spa with your pool. A spa can either be located outside, with the pool, or enclosed in a nearby pool house, which could have the added benefits of sheltering the pool and providing an ideal habitat for warmth- and humidity-loving plants. A popular family-style plan is for a hot water spa adjacent to the cooler refreshing pool; any overflow from the spa can go directly into the pool.

• Waterfalls can be planned when siting your pool. They look very pretty and add sound and movement to the entire garden. While you are in the mood, design your waterfall with your children's fun in mind. Wouldn't they just love a waterfall with a secluded 'secret pool' behind it, where they could hide and play? Some of the fantasy pools in holiday resorts can be imitated — how about a slippery slide, an underwater passage or a knotted rope that can be used as a 'Tarzan' swing?

• Plan a poolside structure of some sort to provide a shaded retreat from the sun, as well as

pool site and choosing your pool. Remember the unofficial Murphy's law of pool design: There will be a drain or electricity cable exactly where you want to put the pool!

It is wise to take the time to contact your local council and ascertain what restrictions apply to pools and poolside structures in your area. Most local codes are fairly straightforward, specifying items such as maintenance of water quality and the provision of safety equipment. However, there are certain areas where council regulations differ quite a lot, notably height restrictions on childproof fences, how close to property boundaries you can build, and lot coverage (the amount of your land that you can cover with a pool and/or paving).

Recently, a number of children have drowned tragically in unfenced backyard swimming pools, prompting pressure on local and state government bodies for additional control. At present, the majority of Australian

By growing climbing plants over the safety fence around this swimming pool, privacy has been assured

a storage area for pool cleaning and garden equipment if there is no room in an existing garage or cellar. There are many prefabricated structures suitable for the poolside, such as gazebos and pergolas (see pages 72–4 and pages 53–6). Experiment with ideas for extending the existing roofline from the back of the house using a trellis, louvres, reeds or even woven canvas or plastic, which will provide dappled light and a linking device between the home and the entertaining area.

• What about an ornamental bridge or a fanciful sculpture arching over the pool? This can be a visually pleasing device, creating an impression of mystery and space. It can also have important

Tip

Not everyone's funds will run to a greenhouse, but I know many children who are totally absorbed in their own small greenhouse, growing easy-flowering plants along with cucumbers, eggplants, tomatoes and ornamental gourds.

practical applications separating, for instance, a paddling pool for the children from a long rectangular pool that is suitable for lap swimming.

• There is plenty of pool equipment that can provide children and their friends with fun. Lightweight nets and floating hoops for water volleyball are available in specialist pool stores, for instance; they are simple to install and easy to remove and store when you want to swim. For a little more money, you could buy a fibreglass slide, which is great fun for young children, or a diving board. These two pool accessories *must* be professionally installed for safety's sake; also, check with the store or contractor whether your pool is sufficiently long and deep enough for a diving board, and be sure to ask for a board with a non-slip surface.

Some stores stock a variety of games and accessories for pool recreation, from fancy rings for swimming through and water basketball, to the more humble kickboards and arm floats. Homemade games will also enhance children's enjoyment of their pool — try racing while holding plastic cups with a toy or ball inside held aloft, or 'fishing' for coins or other small metal toys dropped into the shallow end of the pool.

• For the hardworking parents, nothing beats a sauna for relaxing tired muscles before plunging into the cool, refreshing water. Some saunas are available in kit form and can either be assembled by yourself or by a tradesperson. A sauna may be incorporated into a poolside structure, such as a gazebo, or a freestanding structure. Most importantly, give plenty of thought to water safety and to avoiding hazards with your pool. In addition to installing fencing, which will help keep toddlers out of the pool, apply a little common sense with these home safety rules:

1. **Keep glasses — even plastic ones — well away from the pool. One smashed glass can deposit dozens of tiny sharp fragments on the floor of a pool.**

2. **Store all electrical appliances away from the pool. Make sure any extension cords are tracked well away from the water.**

3. **Keep the pool area clean and tidy. Clear away leaves and other debris which can easily become slippery.**

4. **Learn first aid and mouth-to-mouth resuscitation. Even a young child who is a reasonable swimmer can get into difficulties during an exciting game, or float out of his or her depth.**

Fountains, Waterfalls and Watergardens

Water is the soul of a garden — murmuring, gurgling and splashing. It has a presence so powerful that even the interesting assortment of plants is of secondary importance. Still water can produce a feeling of serenity; little ponds surrounded by mossy bricks create the effect of a small oasis and, by installing a comparatively cheap submersible electric pump, a waterfall can provide a strong focal point. The sound of water is as important as the sight of it in a garden. Whether it is the quiet drip or splash of water from a gargoyle's mouth into a stone basin, or a spectacular waterfall cascading into the swimming pool, the sound of falling water will create a cool, calm and private atmosphere even on the hottest and driest day. More prosaically, water is vital for any style of garden, for without it, the plants will die.

As well as the visual and sensory benefits of incorporating a water feature in the family garden, it acts as a magnet for children — watching fish or tadpoles will provide endless enjoyment. Naturally, safety must be considered; children can drown in small, shallow pools and waterfalls. Just as you would build a fence around the family swimming pool, be sure to install a heavy mesh covering just below or right on the surface, or just above the surface of the water when the pond or water feature is being built. When my uncle fitted a grille into his pond he pointed out grimly that he was less concerned about the safety of small children, but more so about his prized golden carp, which were preyed upon by birds and cats.

Meshing is the ideal solution when ensuring the safety of a water feature. It is a simple matter to plant most aquatics, such as *Nymphoides geminata* and other aquatic floating plants like pondweed and eelgrass or ribbonweed. These will provide a safe breeding area for water snails, insects and frogs, and also produce oxygen, essential for healthy pond life. Fish, especially, require oxygen in order to survive. It is important that the water in a fish pond be circulated and, ideally, sprayed through the air as a fountain or waterfall. Additional meshing must be allowed to protect the fish from the mechanics of the water reticulation system and from the suction inlets themselves. Most systems come with prefabricated grilles for this reason but it is important to be aware just in case — I clearly remember an unfortunate gold guppy that was chewed up in the waterworks of our courtyard fountain when I was young.

Another tip to remember: water plants need to be thinned out regularly, otherwise the pond will become choked and stagnant. If excessive 'blanket' weed forms, remove it by pushing a bamboo cane straight into the mass, twisting it around (as you would when eating spaghetti) and then lifting out the clump and putting it in the compost heap. Some plants, like water-lilies, are best grown in pots under the water to control their growth. When planting in containers, place gravel on top of the medium to prevent fish from disturbing it and muddying the water. Top up a pool or bottom basin of a cascade occasionally to make up for increased evaporation during hot sultry weather.

Few gardens will have a pretty stream or rivulet running through them. However, the tranquil effect of water need never be excluded through lack of space. Small wall-fixed fountains will charmingly set off the smallest shady corner. And, in even the most confined spaces, such as in flats or apartments, where only a balcony or window ledge may be available, a simple bird bath will attract small birds. Similar bowls, made of terracotta or a cement mix, can be placed in shrubbery about the garden to provide bathing and drinking sites for birds, provided they are well out of the reach of cats (see pages 165–8).

Even a simple water feature like this one can be a focal point in a small garden

A simple spout or a soft, round or oval pond can be the centrepiece of a paved area, perhaps distracting the eye from an unwanted view of a service area. A selection of both aquatic and moisture-loving plants in and around the water feature will produce a serene and naturalistic effect. I believe it is important that streams and ponds in a garden should attempt to follow the laws of nature. Examine the natural contours of your garden to see what sort of pool forms are suggested. Generally speaking, if a pool or waterfall is intended to look natural, it should be constructed in the lowest part of the garden. Whether the water flows naturally or not, at least it will appear convincing. A fountain will look out of place and rather pretentious perched on top of a hillock in a suburban garden — after all, water is rarely found at the top of a hill! Far better to introduce a fountain to a shady area near a courtyard or pergola where you are likely

to sit on a hot day. Similarly, an artificial stream or waterfall should connect with a calm pool at some point, rather than just endlessly rush nowhere. A swimming pool is the ideal complement. Many swimming pool companies are exploring a wide range of options for families who already have a pool in their backyard, or who have inherited one in a new home. Until recently, the trend was to simply plunk the pool in the centre of the lawn. More modern pool designers try to integrate the pool with an area for entertaining and often use features like waterfalls, rockeries, fountains and even spas to soften the overall effect.

There must be a suitable water supply when pools or ponds are to be constructed. In some areas the domestic supply will be adequate but in others this can prove expensive — or may be restricted — during dry periods. If you are planning on a major water feature project, check that you will be able to have an adequate permanent water supply.

Excavations for ponds, pools or water features should really be dug down to stable

Try to take inspiration from nature when creating a water feature in your garden

foundations for the best results. The excavated soil and rocks can easily be utilised in a nearby rockery or raised flower bed or shrubbery. There are a number of ways to make watercourses and pools waterproof, including clay linings, bitumen, reinforced plastic liners over a layer of packing sand and — most often with varying degrees of success! — the time-honoured do-it-yourselfer's special version of handmixed concrete trowelled into light mesh reinforcement (usually chicken wire). The main advantage of excavating and finishing a pond or water feature in this way is that you do obtain exactly the shape you want. The surface quickly weathers to an unobtrusive shade, especially if a tint or loam is added to the final render.

For large-scale construction of watercourses, ponds or even dams, it is best to call in an expert, who will generally employ the sprayed concrete method (this method is also used extensively for building swimming pools). However, for a simple

family garden water feature, I do not believe you can improve upon the large variety of pre-formed fibreglass or hardened plastic structures which are now widely available. These can be set directly into a prepared hole in the ground, or stepped into a series of drops against a slope or incline if you are designing a cascading waterfall. For the more proficient, plastic liners may be purchased and set along the path of the watercourse, then covered in stones that have been bedded in cement. Again, the advantage is that you can plan your water feature in precise detail, altering its course or creating miniature pools, as you fancy. Whichever method you choose, all the necessary equipment and materials are available from specialist garden suppliers. Provided you are prepared to rope in help from some adult friends, installing a shaped fibreglass pond or cascade can make for an enjoyable, messy and satisfying family day!

If you are constructing a series of pools as

The paved pathway around this pond enables you to wander around its perimeter

part of a waterfall, you will need to allow for overflow and also make allowance for the return of water to the top of the fall. A garden supplier will be able to supply you with a reticulating pump which will be submerged in the bottom pond to convey water back to the top layer.

Ask for expert advice when calculating the volume of water and the flow rate you would like. You may be surprised to learn that, on a windy day, a significant volume of water in a fountain or waterfall will simply be blown away, thus running the risk of the pump running dry and being damaged. It is also important to take into account the splashing of the fountain in adjusting the level of water so it cannot spill over the sides. Give some thought to the power bill when planning a cascade, waterfall or fountain; often, a simpler design will provide just as much enjoyment without being prohibitively expensive.

It is important to stabilise the surrounding area after the water feature is installed. It is relatively simple to introduce a few large boulders around the edges to create short-term security. I particularly like the look of large rocks slightly overhanging the water. Not only does it create interest and design tension, it provides protection and shade for fish and helps maintain an even water temperature. For inspiration, look at illustrations of natural waterfalls. A simple artificial equivalent could see a single large flat stone, sun-warmed, overhanging an urban waterfall, a perfect spot for children to sit and plop pebbles in the water. In keeping with the 'wild' jungle look, set a stand of scented ginger plant (*Hedychium*) or acanthus nearby.

To avoid potentially damaging settlement and erosion over the subsequent months, plant trees, ferns and shrubs around the 'banks'. They will provide roots to bind the subsoil and surface. As soon as is practical, cover any remaining exposed areas with grass, or construct a densely planted rockery. *Cissus antarctica* will cast quite deep shade and soften the look of the feature. Deft plantings of moisture-loving maidenhair fern and *Sticherus flabellifolius* will

Fuchsias are quick-growing and add colour to the edges of a pond

quickly disguise the edges. Other quick-growing plants are ranunculus, scillas, freesias, bluebells, fuchsias and pratias, or the widely popular native violet, *Violet hederaceae*. If space permits, bog iris, Japanese anemone, and bulrushes will provide shelter for birds and frogs.

Many alpines are easy to grow if space is more limited and are most appropriate in a rockery and waterfall combination. They have the appeal of all miniature things and will help to create an illusion of scale on a rocky outcrop as well as producing brightly coloured flowers. Sun-hardened Kurume azaleas are equally suitable, so long as the soil is gritty and free-draining and the position is well away from overhanging trees.

Safety Tip

Fit any rainwater barrels or similar water-collecting areas with a childproof cover. Your child can drown in as little as 5 centimetres of water.

Gazebos and Summerhouses

From Cleopatra's gold cloth pavilion to the exquisite, painted teahouses of ancient China, garden shelters of one kind or another have a long and colourful history. It was the Elizabethans who first created 'summerhouses', distinguished by a great many windows, as part of the plan for majestic country estates. In fact, the word gazebo is a corruption of the phrase 'to gaze about', which finally stuck!

Gazebos were extremely popular amongst the 18th-century English nobility and were often works of art in their own right. Some were Gothic, others Classical in style. A few were made from wood, but most were made of stone or, latterly, cast iron. During the reign of Queen Victoria, these private garden pleasures became a feature in many public parks, where they most often served as a band shelter.

The new interest in gazebos and summerhouses indicates a certain nostalgia. However, whereas the original English concept was of a slightly exotic glassed-in shelter from which to observe a garden, today's gazebo designers prefer to incorporate their open, airy structures into a garden, where they may be used for eating or as a children's playhouse. Many manufacturers provide kit forms, usually of timber and lattice, and of a hexagonal or octagonal design. Most commonly, a bench is incorporated into the gazebo wall, but of course freestanding furniture could be used instead. Gazebos create a feeling of privacy and provide a splendid shady retreat for either parents or children, in lieu of a cubby house. They can

Gazebos create a feeling of privacy for both children and adults

also usefully double as a spot to store garden furniture or equipment, or for tender plants during cooler months.

If you hanker for a gazebo in your garden, you will need to do a little research first. In some areas a permit is required before building any kind of outdoor structure. There are usually very few relevant restrictions. Authorities will only interfere if other people, namely neighbours, are going to be adversely affected.

Consider the design of your garden as a whole and plan to place your gazebo in harmony with your house and also with any other special features, such as paths and existing flower beds. It is sensible to position the gazebo where it will provide shelter from the heat of the sun; it is also desirable to angle it so it is not fully in view of occupants of either your house or your neighbours' house, thus providing privacy for a snooze or a quiet read. A pretty idea is to place a birdbath or sculpture nearby for people in the gazebo to gaze upon. A water feature, such as a pond or a small fountain, is particularly appropriate, creating a tranquil view for the inhabitant of the gazebo. Lattice may be used to screen the sides of the gazebo and it is then easy to train attractive climbing plants over the screen, providing extra shelter and privacy as well as scent and colour.

Ensure you have a suitably level foundation. Obviously a sandy or damp spot will spell disaster. The gazebo should be located where it can take advantage of a summer breeze, but be protected from strong winds, as well as provide an attractive view of the garden. Traditionally, gazebos were always positioned on a grassy knoll (presumably to overlook several hundred acres of lush pasture!). Even if your house is not situated on such generous acreage, the same principle applies: locate the gazebo on a high, rather than low, spot in the garden. This should mean you are building on firm dry soil, rather than on a low-lying damp spot. Even a little height will help to create an aspect in a backyard.

What design do you have in mind for your gazebo? The octagonal or hexagonal styles, usually with a peaked roof, are very popular.

Design your gazebo to blend in with the style of your garden and other fixtures

You might also consider a circular or even an oval gazebo, along the lines of the pavilions or 'follies' of the Edwardian era. To be truly authentic, the inside of the roof should be dome-shaped, and decorated with *trompe l'oeil,* an extravagant painting style usually featuring exotic but realistic scenes from mythology and nature and intended to fool the viewer.

Natural materials, such as wood, lattice and shingle, are presently very popular for constructing gazebos and summerhouses. Though they are very romantic and look lovely when they are overgrown with vines and creepers, they are probably not as sturdy or long-lasting as those that have brick or stone bases and a tiled roof, or at least metal supports. In tropical areas in particular, heavy rainfall and enthusiastic plant growth can bring a gazebo to grief in a few years. As with any permanent construction, it is wise to seek professional advice before building.

A gazebo can be a simple construction, such as this one, or a more elaborate style

A pretty and practical idea is to night-light your gazebo, especially if you plan to eat there on summer evenings. Soft lighting can be concealed behind shrubs, or you can introduce a flight of fancy with strings of fairy lights around and over the roof — children and adults alike will find this a magical idea. In keeping with this romantic mood, give some thought to a path to approach your gazebo. A pretty, curved walkway made from stepping stones will enhance the feeling of intimacy. In old style gardens, a gazebo or summerhouse was often approached via a concealed doorway or a narrow gap in a hedge, which had the added advantage of shielding the occupants of the gazebo from wind.

Tip

The family garden can be a wonderful place to teach children about nature and to encourage them to appreciate its beauty. Encourage them to observe the way foliage and bark change with the seasons and the weather. Let them roll about in freshly cut grass or autumn leaves. Show them how to sit quietly — well, reasonably still, anyway — so they can watch the wonderful world of insects, especially butterflies, and beetles. They will learn that a caterpillar devouring a leaf ten times its own size is at least as exciting as the umpteenth turn on the latest video game!

Rockeries and Rock Gardens

In Victorian times, a rock garden or 'rockery' was likely to be a quite extravagant garden feature. Originally, the aim was to create an area suitable for the cultivation of rare alpine plants, imitating in miniature the mountain scenery from which these plants had come. No expense was spared in bringing together massive quantities of rock and creating scaled-down mountain landscapes, sometimes with bizarre details such as trains and tunnels to make them more authentic.

Today, rock gardens and rockeries more usually provide a background to an interesting display of succulents, small flowering perennials and prostrate trailing or rosette-forming plants or shrubs, which contrast well with the rugged texture of the rocks. Among the many suitable kinds are sempervivums, saxifrages, gypsophila, sedums and many species of dianthus. Alyssum, bright gazanias and cacti are also successful in a rockery or rock garden, though the latter should not be accessible to young children, for obvious reasons. Fissures and cracks between boulders should be left to form shallow soil pockets for planting species of tiny creeping plants and mosses. Examples include *Wahlenbergia gloriosa*, *Hibbertia obtusifolia*, *Goodenia hederacea*, *Tetratheca thymifolia* and *Brachycome aculeata*.

Rockeries may be used as a method of containing enriched soil in gardens that have

A rockery on several levels, containing brightly coloured flowering plants

*Large stone boulders overgrown with creeping plants form
a very natural-looking rockery*

poor soil, as well as separating different kinds of plantings from one another. Rockeries can also be a way of raising beds and providing better drainage. In certain circumstances, small rock gardens can be constructed around the base of small or unstable trees with weak root systems that could easily be uprooted, especially in wet or windy weather. In the latter case, rocks may be used as a form of support, partly buried in the soil over the roots of the susceptible tree or shrub.

The key to successfully designing a rock garden is to place the rocks so they seem to project from the soil, not rest on top of it. Ideally, a rock garden should be built into a bank, thus simulating a natural outcrop. Similarly, local stone is more likely to look right. Natural sandstone boulders look beautiful and encourage the growth of interesting lichens and mosses. Granite boulders also look very attractive in a rockery. Basalt and other volcanic stones often have very interesting pitted surfaces, which can complement the look of a contemporary house featuring plenty of wood and glass. This is also the most appropriate type of rock to use in a Japanese style garden or a water garden, as they look very interesting when they are wet.

Unless rocks are available from your own garden, for example, during excavation, they should only be bought from reputable garden centres and nurseries. Many national parks have been stripped of natural bush rocks by unscrupulous operators. Quite often a trip to the country can yield a supply of rocks; farmers are usually happy to give away rocks they have removed from newly cleared fields, or to charge only a relatively small fee for them.

Natural boulders are most likely to retain their colour and shape. Excavated stones, on the other hand, particularly limestone or marble, are not recommended for rockeries as they are more likely to weather and split, turning a dirty colour and growing mould. They are also highly alkaline and will leach calcium into the soil, which can cause many varieties of plants to fail. Slate and shale may also be used in the rock garden, however, they too, are likely to deteriorate in time.

There are even artificial rocks available at some garden supply stores. These are quite often used as shells to conceal outdoor equipment, pool fixings or even speakers, which can be tracked to an indoor-controlled sound system. Artificial rocks can be made from sand, soil, and cement and moulded into a simulated outcrop. Mounded clay and bagged sand, reinforced and held in place with a layer of chicken wire, can also be used to create a large outcrop of 'rocks' in the absence of real ones. This method is commonly used in large-scale landscaping and can be very successful. Provided care is taken to build up the soil levels around the artificial outcrop, as happens in the natural landscape, the result will give the impression of natural weathering, particularly if fine gravel and loam are scattered over the area. Firstly, this gives the finish a natural tone and, secondly, it quickly supports moss growth, allowing an interesting texture to develop on the rock's surface as the plants become established.

Before arranging your stones, try to remove every trace of weeds. Spread a good layer of crushed stone or roadbase and sand before starting to arrange the rocks. Choose large slabs as cornerstones and build them into the chosen bank or slope of soil, filling in behind each one with some soil and pressing down well. Each stone should be angled back slightly — the idea is to allow rainwater to flow evenly all around the rockery, not to be directed to any one spot, which may cause erosion.

Consider incorporating a pond for fish (see pages 155–8) or a drinking pool for birds as you go. Birds love to splash in shallow, sun-warmed water. Search for a slightly indented rock and

Safety Tip

Fit safety gates to the top and bottom of garden steps if very young children have access to them, with or without adult supervision.

nestle it in the rockery between, say, *Grevillea alpina* and some bright *Helichrysum brachteatum,* which will attract birds. With the foundation layer of stones in position, add a second layer and then a third and/or fourth, setting the faces of these rocks a little further back each time. As you go, work in a good sprinkling of blood and bone and set the roots of trailing and rosette-forming plants in the fissures and pockets, helping to secure the rockery from the start.

Rockeries need regular watering, but this is the one thing that can spell their destruction. Why? A fierce jet of water can easily disturb the soil and dislodge small plants. The solution is to lay a sprinkler system as you build the rockery. This way, a fine spray of water will ensure the plants receive adequate moisture without any risk of overwatering.

Arbours and Archways

Many small to medium-sized established allotments which constitute the basis for a family home and garden are not necessarily well-oriented to the sun or climate. While a complete overhaul of the garden may be out of the question due to financial considerations, small and careful replanning of a few key aspects can change the whole look and feel of the area, thus enriching home life. Arbours and archways are a good example of how introducing a quite small but significant element of garden design will enhance both the house and garden. With a house of a definitive older architectural style, or where a cottage garden effect is being sought, an arbour or archway — usually planted with that sentimental favourite, the old-fashioned rose — are inclusions often seen. And what better place

to sit and enjoy the sunshine while supervising children at play?

Rambling scented roses are ideal for training over an arbour. 'Albertine' has richly scented pink flowers; those of 'Polyantha Grandiflora' are small, pretty and white. Less vigorous but advantageous for their repeat-flowering habit are 'Casino' (yellow) or 'Handel' (pink-tipped white). Camellias, hostas and ivy are other possible choices for planting under and over an arbour. The dainty flowers of the white jasmine, *Jasminum officinale*, have a luscious perfume. Elizabethan poets mention it as being in common use on arbours, for it was introduced from the East during the Tudor period. Ordinary soil suits jasmine well but, for added protection, plant rosemary or lavender at its base. To enhance the fragrance in early summer

A welcoming archway of flowers at the entrance to a charming cottage garden

set one of the night-scented tobacco plants, *Nicotiana affinis*, nearby.

Honeysuckles, also known as woodbine, are a pretty choice for an arbour or archway. Try planting two together at either side; they will climb together to the top. *Lonicera periclymenum* blooms in high summer; 'Serotina', a little later. Perhaps the loveliest of all is *L. japonica* 'Halliana', which has glossy green leaves and fragrant, creamy yellow flowers. Complement it with the pink-tinted flowers and grey foliage of the elegant *L. caprifolium*. The climbing convolvulus has long been popular as a colourful, quick-growing climber that loops over shrubs and bushes. It can become a noxious weed but, if clipped back regularly, will enhance an arbour with its large white funnel-shaped flowers. The blue bindweed or *C. major* 'Purpurea' has brilliant blue flowers, which are a

pleasing foil to the white-flowered variety.

The floor of the arbour may be of gravel, sand, paving or flagstones or, as a finishing touch, you could set a number of chamomile plants (*Anthemis nobilis*) between irregular pieces of paving laid under or in front of an arbour. They give off an aromatic fragrance when crushed but they will not withstand continuous wear, especially if shaded.

'Arbour' most usually refers to an arched trellis for the purpose of training climbing roses to form a freestanding arch over a pathway. A simply constructed arbour may be erected using five sections of lattice painted green or stained with wood preservative. Ask your timber merchant to cut each panel to the size of 2.5 x 1.5 metres — this will give plenty of headroom while allowing for a thick canopy of plants on top. One section will be used for each side, two for the back and one for the 'roof'.

To hold each section in place, drive four 2.8-metre lengths of 5-centimetre square timber or metal rods into the ground. This allows for each to be driven in at least 30 centimetres. To reinforce the 'roof', fix two struts of 2.5-centimetre square timber across the top (at the back and front) and attach the canopy to these. It will take at least two competent people to erect this arbour, even though the actual construction is quite easy.

One of the quickest ways of building a leafy arbour is to utilise an existing tall, thick hedge, brick wall or wooden fence and then station a pair of upright wooden posts at the garden-facing corners of the hedge gap. Weave a 'roof' of stout wire or thick weatherproof rope between the top of the posts and the back. Support and train honeysuckle, clematis or Virginia creeper to form a high, leafy canopy.

'Archway' is more likely to refer to the enormous variety of shaped or prefabricated decorative steel, powder-coated metal, wooden lattice, or mesh structures available from garden supply centres. These are usually created around steel rods and often borrow motifs from the Victorian foundry style of the late 19th century. Depending on the size and shape, a metal arch is more likely to be able to support heavier climbers, such as grape vines, wisteria or a bougainvillea.

Arbours give instant pleasure to everyone who enjoys a quiet moment in a garden. Every garden needs such a secret place of escape, sheltered by cool green leaves and fragrant flowers. Arbours are a gracious structure in which to share the garden with family and friends. Imagine lunch or afternoon tea under your arbour in the heat of summer. And, when not in use, an arbour is an ideal place for storing a collection of shade-loving plants. If possible, build your arbour where there is a view of the whole garden, or in a secluded corner near a shady tree. Ideally the aspect should be west or southwest, to enjoy a beautiful sunset. Consider placing a chair or bench of wood or wrought iron in the arbour. Simple, child-sized stones can

An archway overgrown with climbing plants creates a green, tunnel-like walkway into this courtyard garden

also be used and 'upholstered' with one of the creeping herbs, such as thyme or mint.

Arbours made from trellis were, apparently, favourite garden features in ancient Rome, as proven by frescoes discovered at Pompeii. However, it was in 18th-century France that such arbours were most used, not only to connect small buildings within the garden, but also as a means of disguising ugly walls or background, and to give small gardens the appearance of being larger. Although there is a school of thought which argues that less is more, I must say that it has been our experience — in a small garden which has had to accommodate two exuberant small boys as well as parents who like to potter — that garden features, such as archways and arbours, used with wit and imagination, will actually create the illusion of more space in the garden by forcing the eye to a focal point and creating a false depth perspective.

Similarly, a view framed in a series of arches can be used to great effect in a long garden. No view? A simple garden seat or pot placed centrally, or to one side of an arbour, will help to halt attention and thus slow movement down.

In a *very* small space, you could try creating an 'Alice in Wonderland' mood for children by introducing a *trompe l'oeil* design on the wall behind an arch, or using outsized plants, pots or outlandish ornaments to make a 'folly'. From a design point of view, there is much to be said for emphasising, rather than trying to play down, the size of a small garden. And children just love the deliberate use of strangeness in a garden. Arches become fortresses, pots become hiding places for Ali Baba, and an assorted jumble of dishes and coloured rocks become magic charms to wish upon.

Archways and arbours will help to give your garden that elusive 'third boundary' by creating a 'space within a space'; you can also create an atmosphere that is somehow outside time. A small archway can, for instance, be an essential part of a design for a garden that is dominated by tall buildings or is heavily overlooked, and makes an attractive and relaxing place for you and your children to sit and rest awhile. After all, there is no rule to say that a family-oriented garden cannot contain small intimate spaces which are totally or partially hidden from view of the house and the rest of the garden. Children, just like adults, appreciate opportunities to distance themselves from the world around them on occasion.

Archways and arbours have particular appeal in a deliberately rambling informal garden, filled with luxuriant, tumbling plantings. Bring magic and mystery to the most unprepossessing dark corner of your garden — even the one that leads to the compost bin — by framing it with an arch, partly hidden by taller, ferny plantings in front. In a small front garden, arbours can be a simple two-dimensional threshold, marking the boundary between the garden and the street. In a back garden, or down a shady side passage, an arbour may be 'stretched' to create a three-dimensional walkway of considerable visual delight and perfume. The great advantage of using wooden trellis is that it allows air to circulate and, provided the climbing plants are not completely overgrown, for natural light to penetrate. Its other great virtue is that, no matter how unattractive that particular site within the garden may be, the trellis arbour will create a private enclosed world with a minimum of effort, cost and time.

Outdoor and Rustic Furniture

In the family garden there should always be a firm, flat surface for the area where you would like to position a table and chairs for dining, and also for the larger and more comfortable chairs in which the parents can (hopefully!) simply sit and read the newspaper while the children play. Garden tables and chairs must never wobble. It is dangerous (hot food can slip off a table and a wobbly chair can pinch a child's hand or foot or upend them entirely) as well as irritating.

When planning the area where the garden furniture will be placed (whether it is a courtyard, terrace or shaded part of the lawn) ensure that the proportions are as generous as possible. You will need to allow for the easy movement of chairs when sitting down to or rising from the table. Also consider whether your outdoor furniture will be left outside in all weathers and select materials on that basis. If the furniture is likely to weather poorly you should look around for overnight storage areas, such as a cellar or garage (furniture can be suspended from hooks).

Even in a modest family garden, it is possible to create a landscape that is worth sitting down and looking at. While you possibly do not possess a pond surrounded by colourful plants and inhabited by a clutch of appealing ducklings during spring, there is still bound to be an attractive, preferably sunny, spot where you can enjoy the fragrance of a scented bush. A table and chairs or a freestanding wooden seat can overlook or be positioned right beside a water area or flower bed. They can be placed in a shady green part of the garden, providing a pleasant place to sit and eat and rest from the day's chores. A small walled garden or corner of a garden with a warm and open aspect can become a wonderful suntrap. The wall space may be used for tender climbers or for hanging pots filled with colourful annuals, leaving the central space free for your table and chairs.

Consider the changing seasons; study the pattern of sunlight and shade in your garden, taking into account the longer shadows cast during spring and autumn. It is a simple matter to construct or buy a wooden bench seat and place it against a wall where you might even sit out on a mild winter's day. A secluded, cosy seat

White wrought-iron garden furniture is always popular

can easily be made as a niche in the masonry of a wall as it is being constructed and will rapidly become a favourite hiding place for a child, or a favourite spot for quiet relaxation.

The easiest method of all is to place one or two aged railway sleepers onto offcuts of open-ended large pipes that have been securely wedged into the soil. If building a seat seems a little ambitious, simply build a bench seat against an existing brick or wooden wall or retaining fence, against which you can lean. The wood should be treated with a commercial wood preservative if it is to last well and avoid attacks from termites and other pests. The great advantage of a wooden seat is that it can be moved, if required, and may be made as long or as short as you prefer. A terrific effect may be gained by setting such benches around the edges of a walled courtyard or upper garden level or even into the sides of a sunken mudbrick enclosure around a central barbecue or shady tree. Containers of flowering plants can be placed at the ends of the

seat and changed with the seasons. Such wooden seats are especially striking when placed in a section of the garden where large rocks or a rock garden is situated; weathered wood and stone make an attractive combination.

For a more rustic look, small seats made from tree trunks are perfect

When buying or making furniture, be sure to consider the style of the garden. Furniture should complement the garden's mood and content, just as indoor furniture should suit the personality of the room in which it is placed. Also take into account the type of fencing and gates you have, or plan to have. A wooden picnic setting will probably look more 'at home' with ranch-style rail fencing or other wooden fencing (see pages 11–12). I tend to think that garden seats should look as though they grew in the garden, just as the plants have done. For a comfortable, family-oriented, welcoming garden, look for styles and materials in garden furniture that will weather gracefully. Only in a more formal garden, where an attempt is being made to match a period style, should elaborate period-style furniture be used.

A wooden table and chairs or benches would blend well with lush plantings of Australian native plants and ferns. Light bench seats of red gum set on heavier sections of railway sleepers will weather to a soft dove grey and make charming informal seating in, say, a barbecue area. Even well-located fallen logs can be a very comfortable spot to sit and can be particularly suitable for a casual style garden. California redwood, western red cedar, jarrah (*Eucalyptus marginata*), oak and treated pine are all used to manufacture a wide variety of settings, chaise longues, benches, recliners, planter boxes and other accessories. The important thing to remember about any timber furniture is that it should be strong and durable when left outside. Outdoor furniture that will last without having to be painted or stained every year has a decided advantage. However, most manufacturers usually recommend an annual coat of linseed oil or a similar wood preservative for continued protection.

Wooden furniture is pleasantly informal and lovely to sit on. Be sure to sand back any rough sections so that bare-legged children do not get splinters. Lightweight concrete is another

A stone table and bench seats would look particularly attractive in a paved courtyard garden

Things to Do

Beans and peas germinate quickly, making excellent subjects for indoor gardening and simple nature experiments for children. Take a round, wide-necked jar and run a thick fold of blotting paper around the inside. Slot a few beans or peas between the paper and the glass and then pour a little water in the bottom of the jar so the blotting absorbs it, at least to the height of the beans and peas. Within a few days the seeds will germinate, the shoots growing up and the leaves developing, and the roots growing downwards for anchorage.

alternative. Artificial 'rocks', made from chicken wire shapes coated with concrete can be used as seating. So, too, can real rocks, of course. Large, smooth, sun-warmed boulders are an idyllic place to sit and play. White or pastel-coloured plastic and mesh or tubular PVC furniture contrasts well with the lush green of a tropical garden or a colour-filled courtyard setting. Plastic outdoor furniture and accessories are particularly recommended for poolside use. Glass-topped tables are elegant, but not a practical choice when you have children. I clearly remember, when I was small, the little boy from next door sitting on top of my mother's glass-topped coffee table which was outside on the terrace. He meant no mischief, but was very lucky to escape with only a few cuts.

New cast-iron or cast-iron and wooden benches made to original Victorian styles are available from many manufacturers. They are very fashionable and look charming in a period-style garden. A diligent search through secondhand stores or demolition sites can yield original curved iron framework supports, though the wooden planking is usually missing. Unless the ironwork is too badly corroded it can be repaired by welding, and replacing the wood is an easy matter. Cast aluminium or steel frame designs are cheaper, however, be sure to check that such products have been galvanised and are guaranteed to resist rusting.

A heavy stone or marble table can have a strong quality in a garden, particularly when placed on top of two fanciful pilasters. Too expensive, you say? Not at all. Lovely lengths of wholly or partially planed stone or marble can be bought direct from stonemasons for a very reasonable price. Similarly, pilasters, plinths, pedestals and other decorative stonework can be purchased at auctions or, if you are lucky, even picked up from demolition site sales. For comfort's sake, wooden benches or seats should be used with a stone- or marble-topped table. Stone benches can look wonderfully appealing, but are far less comfortable. Position them where you may not want to sit on them, so moss or lichens can grow attractively on their surfaces.

Naturally, a stone table and benches are fairly permanent so make sure you are happy with the potential site before putting everything together. I would suggest that a stone or masonry table or benches should be at least partially shaded during summer; being a good conductor of heat they could, quite literally, become too hot to handle, let alone sit upon! My own view is that wooden furniture usually looks better when used among plants, resting on earth or grass; stone tables, on the other hand, suit the architectural setting of a terrace or walled garden.

Statuary, Sundials and Urns

Along with pools and arbours, urns, statues and sundials are traditional ornaments of the garden. Even a small garden can be given a stylish touch with the addition of a small urn or elegant statue.

From a design point of view, a raised feature or statue placed towards the foreground will draw attention to that area and, by shortening this foreground view, will create a greater sense of depth behind. Similarly, placing a fine urn or pot centrally, or to one side and about halfway down a long path, will help to halt attention and thus slow the movement of the eye around the garden. Most often a piece of arresting statuary or other focal point is used to distract the eye from an unwanted view. Statues and sculptures may also

*Small statues of birds and
animals hidden around the garden
will delight children*

Of course, the choice of a distinctive
ornament is completely up to the individual and
the whole family can have fun ringing the
changes and putting their personal stamp on the
garden. After all, is the five-year-old's choice of a
brightly coloured frog peering from a tangle of
shrubs any less effective than an elegant sundial
positioned as a focal point by the pergola? And
there are few gardeners who, no matter how
proficient, do not have a lucky pebble or even a
little weathered gnome quietly sitting somewhere
in the garden, just for luck.

be used as part of a design for a pool or
fountain, perhaps spouting water or
mounted in wall niches. Statues and
sculptures must be able to be viewed
with comfort — near a sheltered sitting
place is usually a nice choice.

It is important that ornaments like
these should not dominate the family
garden, nor should they ever give the
impression that the garden has been
designed around them. Marble statues
of the human figure (which carry very
strong impressions of formal European
gardens) can look quite out of place in
a family garden. Contemporary
sculpture, on the other hand, tends to
marry well with the colours of native
foliage and the peculiarly sharp, bright
light of the Australian landscape.
Importantly, a statue or sundial must
be weather-proof; look for stone,
brick, brass, bronze, iron, copper,
artificial stone or concrete. Be wary of
amateur ceramics as they can become
very fragile. Certain wood carvings
seem to complement the family garden
very well, in particular the weathered
masks and carved poles of New
Zealand and the Pacific Islands look
very much at home in a small clearing,
surrounded by native plants.

*The designer of this garden has created a focal point with this
large urn filled with a flowering plant*

Best of all, children love surprises in a garden and, because in a strange way statues do suggest other presences in the garden, they will satisfy children on this score. They are probably less likely to be curious about dramatic artefacts and may even be quite scared of a blustering or heroic style of statue, but a shepherd with a crook or a pretty wall-mounted cherub surrounded by a ruff of spread wings will both make charming features that the children should find very lovable. Place the statue or piece of sculpture with special care; tucking a small figurine just behind a screen of ferns is far more appealing to children. When they do discover it, there will be the tantalising feeling that they have been watched without knowing it.

Urns, vases and large jars or pots are very adaptable and can probably be used in a great number of places within the family garden rather than statuary or sculpture. Although the average family garden is not really designed along the grand, pathlike scale, urns can still be used very simply on low garden walls to emphasise, for instance, an opening to another part of the garden. Large pots or urns draw the eye and can provide an attractive vertical feature to relieve rather flat areas of garden. A pair of containers is commonly used to mark the foot or head of steps or to decorate entrances or exits.

When selecting an urn or a pot, it is important to keep in mind a sense of the scale of your garden and its style. The natural harmony of the garden can be ruined by ornaments that are too big, too small, or over- or under-stylised. Most nurseries stock a

Things to Do

Children love things that are a bit weird or odd. And what could be odder than a square tomato? Secure a 4-centimetre square clear plastic box (from a gift shop or craft supplier), having cut a small hole in the base to insert over the flower stem, over a green tomato as it starts to grow inside the old flower. Glue or tape the lid of the box back on and use a rubber band or string to loop around the box and tie it to the main stem of the tomato plant, or the stake itself, so it does not sag. Once the tomato has filled the box, carefully take off the lid and cut it up for neat sandwiches!

very wide range of concrete or terracotta pots and urns that are simple in outline and reasonably uniform in colour. These are excellent containers for geraniums, camellias, or even lemon trees and clipped box. I particularly like the look of trailing plants, such as lobelia, ivy-leafed geraniums or trailing convolvulus which spill over the rim of the urn and soften the look. Always consider the requirements of the plants you wish to grow and use an appropriate potting mix.

Ornamental pots and urns may also be made from plastic, stone, simulated stone, concrete or lead-packed fibreglass-reinforced resin. Some very cheap 'antique' lookalike plastic pots are now made by coating the urn or pot with primer and adhesive and rolling it in a coating of ground stone. Both these and the fibreglass pots are extremely lightweight, allowing great ease of movement. However, my preference is terracotta pots or urns, which 'breathe' better than plastic or fibreglass ones, thereby reducing the risk of fungal disease attacking your precious plants. All pots or urns must be planted up carefully and watered regularly or the soil will dry out very quickly. A good tip for the family gardener is to fill urns or pots with soil and plant them and resist the temptation to use them just as ornaments — filled pots are far less likely to be overturned and smashed during active outdoor play.

A sundial can be an amusing garden ornament. The classical sundial, perched on top

of a single column, was enormously popular in formal or semi-formal Edwardian gardens. In fact, many gardens were designed around the sundial, located for maximum sun, rather than the other way around. Even though they keep time precisely, and are perfectly functional in fine weather, sundials are generally bought for ornamental purposes these days. They are usually either the Classical style already mentioned, or a formal shape, like books or crosses, with bronze arrows or highly ornamented pointers (gnomons). As far as the family-oriented garden goes, a formal sundial is probably best placed in the centre of a display flower bed, where it is least likely to be knocked over.

I like sundials and I like the idea of being able to teach children about time and the movement of the sun without a digital flashing light. I also like the idea of a sundial as a family heirloom, being passed down over the years from family garden to family garden, perhaps even embellished with the family's name, coat of arms or motto. Give some consideration to a well-mounted example, or one which can be cemented into a rockery where all the family can enjoy charting the progress of each day. There are even some wonderful giant-sized models that are designed for complete involvement by children: they walk over them and tell the time by looking where their own shadow falls!

To ensure the accuracy of your sundial, it must be located in full sun. In the southern hemisphere, this means it should be positioned on the north side of the building and, in the northern hemisphere, on the south side. In either case, check for large trees or shrubs in any direction which could throw shadows across the sundial.

The Clipped Accents of Home Topiary

We do not know who first used shears to clip trees into fantastic shapes of carved vegetation. Illustrations of an Egyptian garden from around 1400 BC shows rows of date palms shaped into perfect cones on single trunks; is this a fine array of tonsured trees or simply a stylised picture? What we do know is that after Caesar's return to Rome from Egypt, the fashion for clipping bushes became very popular.

In classical Latin, *opus toparium* was a general term to describe the art of ornamental gardening and the *toparius* was the gardener. The term 'topiary' is now generally applied to the cultivation of trees and shrubs that are clipped to zoomorphic or geometric shapes. Sometimes the term is used more loosely to include related techniques such as pleaching and Japanese bonsai. Even pinch-pruning of indoor or outdoor plants to create decorative forms is sometimes described as 'topiary'.

Traditional topiary and other forms of training provide scope for a wealth of designs, ranging from the severely geometric or the adventurously contemporary to the unapologetically whimsical. Imagination is the most important tool and, of course, this is where children can contribute, for even inexperienced gardeners can quickly learn how to train fast-growing vines over simple wire frames placed in containers. Perhaps your family would fancy an elegant green dragon of variegated ivy in the hallway? Or a mischievous monkey hanging from a palm tree in the sunroom? Or perhaps a classical geometric form such as a pyramid,

A pair of neatly clipped trees on either side of a stairway

corkscrew, standard or 'poodle' ball of close-clipped box, juniper or yew? Silhouetted or backlit against a wall in a dining room or lounge, these instantly become a talking point.

FANCIFUL SHAPES

With pre-formed, portable topiary, wire frames are filled with long-fibre sphagnum moss. Then ivy (*Hedera helix*), baby's tears (*Soleirolia soleirolii*) or dracaena (*Dracaena marginata*) are planted in the frame to give the desired effect. Other creepers and flowers popular in pre-formed topiary are the creeping fig (*Ficus pumila*), Corsican mint (*Mentha requienii*), pennyroyal (*Mentha pulegium*) or string-of-hearts (*Ceropegia woodii*). Dwarf aluminium plant (*Pilea cadierei*) can be interplanted with silvery fittonia (*Fittonia verschaffeltii*) for a very pretty effect. Ask a florist or local nursery for suggestions and try experimenting with different shapes and textures, for instance, miniature bromelaids can be used for an unusual decorative 'studded' effect, provided special care is taken not to let them dry out.

Whether making a life-sized peacock or a simple circular wreath, the basic design element is the hoop, made from bent wires — coathanger wire is a good, inexpensive choice — to form the curved shapes of topiary. Trained plants need regular grooming and clipping when necessary. Watch for pests like aphids or mealybugs which love warm, wet moss or bark. Spray with pyrethrum, or dab individual bugs with a cotton bud dipped in rubbing alcohol. Similarly, any mould or fungal diseases can be eradicated by drenching the topiary in a solution of mild fungicide.

An even simpler and very effective variation on a pre-formed shape is to omit the moss and 'plant' the hollow frame into a pot with a plant

that has a good trailing habit, such as the ivy 'Goldheart'. Position the frame securely in the pot. Gently and evenly tie the runners over the frame. Use tiny twist-ties, soft raffia or unobtrusive bits of string. Do not tie them too tightly to the frame or the plant will not be able to grow. As it grows, tying may no longer be needed, just weave and twine the stems around each other.

The elegant lines of potted ivy spirals look equally at home on a country kitchen table as a marble plinth. To make a spiral, take a well-branched ivy plant and securely drive a central vertical stake (a fine wooden curtain rail is ideal) into the bottom of a soil-filled pot. Tie sturdy wire on the stake at soil level and shape the spiral, going from the widest dimension at the bottom and winding it in decreasing coils to allow clear clipping later, when the ivy has grown. At the top of the spiral, fix one end of wire to the top of the stake. Tie the ivy's branches loosely to the wire shape, trimming them with scissors as necessary. A spectacular effect can be created by using different ivies; try using 'Gold Dust' with one of the newer, frilly-leafed varieties.

If a solid mat of leaves is desired, wrap the frame with chicken wire. This will give the stems an opportunity to cluster thickly together. A pretty choice for this method is the honey-scented wax plant, or hoya, with its clusters of rosy flowers. Try training this over a heart-shaped frame for a little girl's bedroom. Provided it is spelled outside in a sheltered, warm position, it should do well. Another fun idea is to cut shapes from chicken wire, using pattern pieces for children's stuffed toys as a guide, before 'stitching' them together with fine florist's wire and using them as the base for leafy puppies, kittens, clowns and many more.

> ## Tip
>
> Special occasion coming up? Dress your shaped plant as guest of honour. Give it an extra soaking so it is well-dampened, then pin flowers and coloured ribbon to it as a festive touch. The damp sphagnum moss will keep them fresh and bright all night.

These rows of clipped trees balance the sharp, clean lines of the entrance to this house

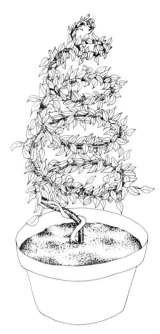

It is easy to create an attractive ivy spiral for either indoor or outdoor use. Simply train ivy or other climbing plants to grow over a spiral made from fairly strong wire. The base of the spiral should begin near the roots of the plant, in the centre of the pot.

When selecting plants for pre-formed topiary, it is best to start with several small plants, rather than one large one. That way you will not have to wait as long for a fully-covered result, and if one plant dies, stems from the others can quickly be trained to cover up the bald patch.

Garden centres and craft supply shops are treasure troves when looking for a pot to best display trained plants. Clay or terracotta containers are preferable to plastic ones as they allow the plant's roots to breathe better and, being heavier, are less likely to topple over. Choose a pot that is a little wider in diameter than the frame is at its widest point.

At least six months to two years is required to create a dense, healthy standard suitable for bringing indoors, so if you hanker for this kind of topiary, visit a specialist nursery. Japanese or English box and yew (*Taxus baccata*) are popular choices for standards. If colour is a key requirement, you could try your hand at shaping cumquats or azaleas. Fuchsias or bougainvillea can be trained as weeping standards; they prefer a sunny aspect. Standard New Zealand Christmas bushes are a wonderful way of brightening the home in time for the Christmas season, their green leaves and fluffy red flowers are perfect for Christmas.

Hardier and equally endearing are herbal topiaries. Thyme (*Thymus vulgaris*), sage (*Salvia officinalis*) and lavender (*Lavandula officinalis*) can be trained to just about any size and shape. Some people like to have them on a kitchen bench or window sill where they may be savoured for their aesthetic and culinary appeal. Rosemary (*Rosmarinus officinalis*) is probably the safest bet for training as a miniature indoor standard. Its fine leaves are a little like those of yew in that they respond well to regular clipping and shaping.

A fashionable choice for an elegant standard is the New Zealand tea tree (*Leptospermum scoparium*). For that matter, roses can be charming, too. Extremely striking — though very time-consuming — is the American variation on basic standard topiaries, the braided standard, in which three plants are set close by each other in the centre of a pot. The central stems or trunks are loosely plaited together with all central branches pinched off and the top growth shaped into a single full head.

Experts say topiary should be given regular sun baths or it will be unhappy. One week in, one week out, will keep most of them healthy. A good idea is to have a pair which can be swapped around periodically.

Tip

Children will enjoy writing their name with plants. Simply trace their name or initials in the soil and densely sow with seeds of Virginia stock or mustard and cress. Water in well and wait for their name to appear.

Window Sills and Window Boxes

Window boxes serve the dual purpose of brightening the facade of a house, as well as the view from within. Growing plants in window boxes is an enjoyable and appealing family project. For some, it is a necessity because they live in a flat and have no garden; for others, window boxes are an interesting and attractive accessory to a 'normal' garden. As a bonus, those who live on alkaline or limestone soils may indulge their interest in lime-hating plants, such as dwarf rhododendrons, through the use of window boxes. Apart from being decorative, window boxes can be very practical. Witness the ones so prevalent in Mediterranean countries, spilling over with healthy fresh herbs that can be easily picked for cooking.

Most plants will do well in window boxes, provided they are neither over-exposed to wind nor completely shaded. Suitable containers can be planted out with bright flowers or even fruit, such as strawberries, and different kinds of small vegetables and herbs. Drought-resistant herbs, such as thyme, rosemary, sage and oregano make particularly good plants for sunny window boxes.

For children, growing a few vegetables in a window box can be fun and the rewards of 'growing their own' are bound to be appreciated. Dwarf French beans and Tiny Tim tomatoes are relatively easy to grow. There is also the advantage that young plants can be bought and placed straight into the container, which is helpful for those with no garden shed where they may raise plants from seed. Children will find the rapid growth of scarlet runner beans most gratifying. In no time at all, they will grow right up to the curtain rod and probably around it, too! Scarlet runner beans will produce giant pods and, inside each pod, children will be delighted to find the same bean they started with. (This project is really only suitable for older children as both the pods and the beans are poisonous, though they may be eaten if cooked first.) Peas, beans and lentils are also fun to watch because

they sprout and grow so quickly. Children can name the different seedlings and have races!

Pelargoniums are excellent subjects for a sunny window box as they will survive for a day or two without water. The trailing ivy-leafed type, such as the pale pink 'Madam Crousse' or the red and white splashed 'Rouletta' are both excellent for a summer display. The old-fashioned scented geraniums, with their various fragrances of lemon and rose, peppermint, musk, almond, apple and nutmeg, will provide much pleasure, especially for children who love to crush and sniff the leaves. Drought resistant Cape daisies (*Felicia bergerana*) and bright yellow gazanias will do well, but you should avoid petunias, impatiens and lobelia if the window boxes are to be exposed to a good deal of sun and/or wind. Other plants which are recommended for window boxes include begonias, English daisies, dianthus, coleus,

Pelargoniums are easy to grow and bring lots of colour to a window box

nasturtiums and spring-flowering bulbs, such as tulips, crocus and narcissi. The handsome Scarborough Lily (*Vallota* spp.) is a very striking plant with its large clusters of red flowers. Pick off flower heads as they fade to maintain a clean and colourful effect.

Many alpines do well in window boxes — their native habitat being dry rock ledges, anyway — and children in particular are fascinated by tiny treasures like *Sempervivum* spp., *Saxifraga cochlearis* and *Origanum amanum.* Cacti, being tough and hardy, are also favoured for a window sill garden. They would need to be kept well out of reach of younger children, of course, but older children tend to find cacti fascinating. Christmas cactus (*Zygocactus*) with its flat, segmented stems and garish pink or red flowers will lend a rakish air to a window sill. The rather revolting Rat's Tail cactus, with its long, hairy, dangling stems, is much admired by small boys, I have found. The South American Pebble Plant (*Lithops*) is another appealing little

oddity which will suit a sunny window sill in a child's room. They may also be intrigued by *Lithops optica* or the window plant, which is almost entirely buried in the soil apart from a little translucent 'window' on the surface which allows light to reach the plant.

It is not difficult for a reasonably competent handyperson to make wooden window boxes. Given that drying out in windy weather is the main problem with them, they should be made as large as possible — a minimum recommended depth, for instance, would be 25 centimetres. Steer clear of tiny or shallow window boxes; the smaller the container, the higher the maintenance. Larger boxes will allow the plants more room for root growth and moisture retention. The box may be filled directly with soil and compost, but it will last much longer if plants are either grown in a plastic trough placed inside the wooden outer, or grown in separate small pots and arranged in window boxes, with a mulch such as bark chips.

Alternatively, line the boxes with zinc or other metal (not copper) or with heavy duty plastic sheeting which will help both prolong the life of the box and retain moisture in the soil. Be sure to provide drainage holes in the metal or plastic to allow excess water to escape. In either case, remember that the window box, once filled with soil, is going to be heavy. Strong metal brackets fixed securely to the wall beneath the window ledge are safe and permanent.

Many different types of decorative window boxes are available from garden centres. As well as boxes of hardwood and treated softwood, there are other kinds made of metal, fibreglass, plastic, concrete, terracotta and reconstituted stone. Terracotta planter boxes are very popular for windows that have a wider than average sill. For safety's sake, you must either chock it up with blocks of wood or bolt it to the sill with steel bolts so it does not fall on anyone beneath. The size and shape of the windows and the architectural style of the house itself will determine the style of window box you select.

Most window boxes come with either sturdy brackets or steel hooks and eyelets. They may either be attached directly to the window frame or hung underneath the window sill or fixed to the wall. If in doubt about the degree of support, be sure to install additional 'insurance', particularly if the window box juts out over a street or garden where it could possibly fall straight onto the head of someone unfortunate enough to be passing beneath. As a safeguard, a chain can be placed around the front of the box and fixed to hooks in the wall, or use heavy duty galvanised straps to attach the window box to a balcony railing, allowing one strap each 30 centimetres for the width of the box.

Things to Do

Show children how to create 'magic', crazily coloured flowers, just for fun. Take a white rose and split the stem down the middle, putting one half in a glass of clear water and the other in a glass with green or bright blue food colouring. Half the stem will suck up the coloured water and half the plain, resulting in a striped rose.

There are two other points to remember for wooden window boxes, whether you have bought one or made it yourself. Firstly, paint it thoroughly, using two coats of primer and an all-weather exterior paint, preferably in a gloss or varnish finish. Be sure to paint both the inside and the outside to minimise the risk of the timber rotting. The inside of wooden boxes should also be treated with a preservative, such as Bordeaux mixture. Avoid creosote, which will damage plant roots. Secondly, make sure the boxes have adequate drainage. Some quite beautiful boxes do not have any drainage holes and it is a simple matter to punch or drill some in the base, thus avoiding an unattractive display of sick plants. Before filling window boxes, cover the drainage holes with fibreglass flywire mesh (available at any hardware store), to prevent potting mix dripping out of the box and down the wall of the house or, worse still, onto people below.

The most important thing to remember about plants in window boxes is to keep them watered. Daily watering may be necessary in warm, dry weather and using a liquid fertiliser once a week will also be useful once flowering has begun. Remember that most window boxes are overhung either by eaves or the window ledge of the flat above and therefore receive very little rain and will need watering, even in wet weather.

Remember also that many of the worst garden pests, such as red spider mites and scale, thrive in warm conditions and are especially bad on plants that have been kept dry at the roots. 'Stir' the soil surface of the plants with a skewer or old kitchen fork occasionally to allow aeration. Potting mix in window boxes tends to get compacted and form a hard crust. Ideally, the soil should be changed completely each year.

3

CHILD'S PLAY

Sandpits and Sandboxes

For a children's play area, a sunken sandpit is easily constructed and will provide hours of pleasure for a very modest outlay and small amount of effort on your part. In the family garden, a soft — but tough — lawn is probably the most important element. However, most children will go through a stage where they are more fascinated by sand than grass and are preoccupied with games that involve building things. It is then that they are most likely to appreciate a free play area that has sand in it in which they can allow their imaginations to take over.

The best spot for a permanent sandpit is in a sheltered position that is open or in dappled shade in summer. Bushy shrubs with soft foliage around the sandpit will satisfy this need and make good hiding places, as well.

Left: A sandpit or sandbox is always a welcome addition to the family garden. A portable model affords you the convenience of moving the sandpit to various locations in the garden

The sand itself should be a clean, well-drained and easy to handle type (which usually means it has a high clay content — check with your supplier). You will need to find a type that will stick together enough so as to be suitable for building castles, boats and roads without collapsing. And, to reduce the likelihood of unseemly yelling later on (I speak from experience) *do* check that the sand does not stain and washes off easily.

Another good tip is to look for sand that is quite coarse. That makes it less likely to stick to clothes. Also, if your sandpit is not likely to be covered all the time it is not in use, ask the supplier for a type of sand which will not bog or harden after rainy weather. Nearly all sands will pack down to a solid mass in such conditions, so do consider a roof or lid for the sandpit. An angled roof can be positioned over an open air permanent sandpit, or the sandpit can be built under a pergola in the first place. A roof or lid will keep the sand smelling fresh by allowing it to breathe. Excessively dry and windy conditions, on the other hand, can make the sand blow away

A sandpit or sandbox will give hours of enjoyment to children

all over the garden, so the pit or box should be misted regularly during warm dry weather.

If you are opting for a portable model, such as one of the lidded moulded plastic sandboxes on the market, you have the advantage of being able to rotate its position regularly, giving the surrounding bits of grass a chance to regrow.

One word of warning though; children have an annoying habit of quickly tiring of most commercially available equipment which is, after all, only an adult's idea of what *they* think children need. Try to seek out the appealing models from the uninspiring. One good example is the hardened plastic shell- or car-shaped sandboxes available through discount shops and department stores. These allow for extra initiative and imaginative play and can double up as paddle pools for very small children, and also have the advantage of being able to be securely covered at night, reducing the likelihood of neighbourhood cats fouling it. The simplest cat-proof cover of all is a piece of shadecloth or weed matting, tacked between two rods, dropped over the sides of the box or pit by night and rolled up when the children wish to use the sandpit.

For parents, the installation of a sandpit is going to be an example of the role of compromise in the family garden. A garden which children will like to use is bound to be a different one from that enjoyed by adults for quite sedentary pursuits, like reading the newspaper. A sandpit full of empty ice cream containers will probably seem extremely squalid to an adult's eye. However, try to remember that beauty is in the eye of the beholder and that a sandpit — above all other garden features — can really turn the family garden into a cheerful, imaginative place full of things to do and ways to have fun that children will remember all their lives.

The sandpit should not be positioned out of sight just because it may appear untidy. It should be near enough to the house so you can keep an eye on them, but not so close that the children's privacy is threatened. Simple screening with climbing plants or shrubs will separate but not isolate the area. When the children are grown and busy with activities that take them away from the family garden, which will be all too soon, the sandpit can be converted to other purposes, such as a compost area, or rockery.

If you are not keen on a commercially produced sandbox, you could try building your own. This can be either a simple pit dug into the

ground, lined with heavy duty shadecloth, weed matting or plastic, pierced with drainage holes before being filled up with sand, or a wooden sandbox. Whether you elect to dig a pit or build a box, the area should be at least 2 metres square to be useful and to provide space for more than one child. Start with six pieces (2.5 centimetres x 30 centimetres x 2 metres) of either cypress pine flooring or redwood planking. The latter is more expensive, but also more likely to be stronger and more weather resistant in the long run. Select a fairly level spot and dig holes for four 60-centimetre high corner stakes (5 centimetres square). Notch four boards up to 15 centimetres at their narrow ends so that they will interlock in a tongue-and-groove style. A handsaw, portable saw or table saw can be used to notch the timber. If a portable saw is used, a protractor or similar device plus a rule should be used to ensure notches are equal and accurately cut to ensure that they lock together smoothly.

Dig a shallow trench between the four corner stakes. Lock together the frame of the box and drop it into the trench. (You will definitely need a partner for this step.) Firm around the wall with earth and tamp down securely. Clamp boards together at corner stakes and use galvanised or steel screws or bolts to secure. For extra security, insert a further four stakes at the outside of each corner and use cross-bolts to screw boards to each stake. Using first a coarse grade and then very fine grade sandpaper, smooth off any rough edges or splinters, inside and out.

To make seats on top of the sandpit, screw the remaining two planks to the top of two sides, securing underneath with cut wood and metal brackets. Ensure there are no protruding bolt ends or nails. Finally, fill the box with sand.

> **Tip**
> ___
> For children who prefer to grow flowers, annuals like portulaca, sweet alyssum and lobelia will survive an amateur scatter-planting and grow practically anywhere. Nasturtiums have nice fat seeds which quickly germinate to form a colourful display, too.

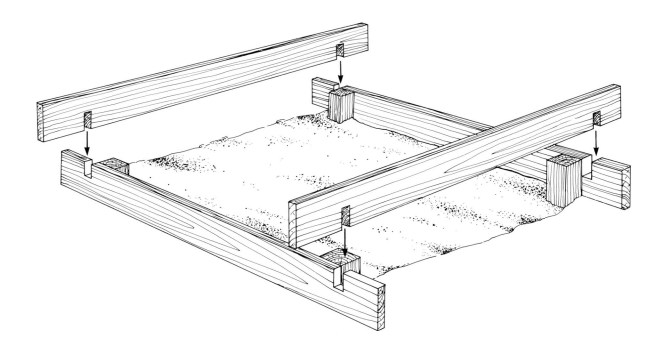

1. On a level spot, dig holes for the four corner posts.
2. Notch the four cross planks so they will interlock,
as shown.
3. Dig a trench between the corner stakes and drop the
sandbox into the trench, then secure the interlocking
joints with bolts. Firm down the soil around the frame
of the sandbox (a further four stakes can be placed at the
outside of each corner for extra security). Fill with sand.

Alternatively, use 12 pieces (three for each side) of 2 metres x 10 centimetres cypress pine flooring or redwood planking and notch the ends, top and bottom, so they will interlock, log cabin style. Treated pine half-logs (say, four to six on each side) are another good choice and will withstand plenty of rugged play. They may be purchased pre-notched for easy assembly, using kit instructions. Kits like these are a good investment for the family gardener because the logs can either be used in the ground to make a sandpit play area or may be moved at a later date, to provide the basis for a playhouse or slide.

The easiest sandbox of all to build is made from just four railway sleepers. These can be obtained through both garden design companies and lumber yards which have access to recycled timber. Using chalk or string, plot the outline of the sandbox on the ground and dig around it to a depth of about 5 centimetres. Either set railway sleepers directly into the trough and secure them at the corners with a good quality weatherproof wood cement, or first bolt and glue the four sleepers together in a frame and then drop this into the depression. It can then easily be filled with sand.

Swings and Other Play Equipment

wings, slides, monkey-bars and seesaws are always favourites with children and provide many hours of fun. After all, every child dreams of being able to fly! Playgrounds often provide swings, but you can easily rig up your own in your backyard cheaply and simply, especially if there is a sturdy tree. Rather than risk having children clambering up onto garage roofs or pretending to 'walk the tightrope' down the fences which divide you and your neighbours' gardens, adults should just make the best of this natural urge and try to make sure a safe, self-propelled flight is available in the form of a swing. And, if your garden simply does not have the right type of tree, you can always purchase a brightly coloured metal frame swing, or one of wood in kit form, which you can assemble and bolt together yourself.

Many swings with metal frames require concrete footings, even if the manufacturer does

As this swing shows, play equipment does not have to clash with the style of your garden

not recommend them; remember that those with wooden frames can also be strengthened with concrete footings. In particular, if the soil in your garden is very light and sandy, it may not be able to support posts or hooks sunk into the ground. If this is the case, you had definitely better investigate securing a framework swing in the ground with concrete footings.

For safety reasons it is advisable to either hang or build your swing over grass or sand, rather than concrete. A fall of only 30 centimetres onto concrete is needed to achieve a 50G impact, that is, 50 times the fall of gravity, which can have the potential to cause concussion in a child. In the spirit of compromise, try to ensure that the swing is not going to be positioned over the nicest stretch of lawn; it will not stand up to scuffing and tumbling. Of course, if you have purchased a swing on a frame, you can rotate its position, giving the worn bits a chance to regrow before the roots are destroyed. Position the rope so that even at full swing there is no risk of the child hitting another object, such as a wall or the tree itself. Keep the area in front of the swing clear for children to jump when getting off.

The most important thing to remember is to avoid tying a rope or chain directly around a branch. It is an easy matter to knot or splice rope around a branch but there is a risk that this could cause ringbarking, or even cause a welt that will let in infection and possibly kill the whole tree. It is far better to drill a hole right through the branch and insert a large steel eye-bolt, ring-side downmost, securing it snugly at top and bottom ends with galvanised washers. To ensure the washers are really firm against the branch, you may have to chisel away a little of the surrounding bark and then screw the washers right up into the wood. Again, though it sounds surprising, this is less likely to cause any harm to the tree and will, in fact, reduce the likelihood of infection. The bolt should be positioned fairly close to the point where it meets the tree trunk. If it is too close to the end of the trunk it can cause strain and break the branch.

Once the bolt is secure, it is simply a matter of hanging the swing itself. A knotted rope will do, preferable nylon, as it will weather best. The length of rope needed will obviously vary, however, you should aim to have the bottom edge of the seat (or old car tyre) no lower than 60 centimetres off the ground. One word of warning: never use clothesline or other cheap rope for a swing. Fine chain or strong nylon rope, at least 2 centimetres thick, is necessary.

Other ideas include a T-bar arrangement with a rod, canvas sling, purchased plastic bucket-shaped safety seat or straight plastic bench seat. If you want to make a swing with a wooden seat you will need to insert two eye-bolts in the branch and hang two ropes to tie to either end of the seat. Flat wooden or plastic seats may be purchased, pre-drilled to take the ropes, from some toy stores and garden centres. However, it is a simple matter to make a wooden seat from 2.5-centimetre thick wood or planking. Sand well to get rid of splinters!

Be sure to check the ropes for fraying from time to time, especially where they meet the seat. An old car tyre is probably the best choice if you have very small children as it is so much safer than a wooden seat if pushed without an occupant, and it is easier to cling to. Two other tips: first, have a go on the swing yourself before anyone else does. If it holds your weight, then it will take a child's. Secondly, very small children will appreciate having a low stump nearby to climb up on, grab the swing and jump off.

Of course, as every parent knows, children are perverse creatures. Adults tend to assume they know the type of play equipment children will like. When thinking about the components of your family's garden, remember that although swings, sandpits, climbing ladders and the like provide terrific fun, certain play activities go in and out of favour from time to time. In short, be flexible and make provision for outdoor play equipment to change as your children's needs change. Here are some ideas:

• Creating things is one of the main aspects of play. Large sections of tree trunks, loose logs and chunks of wood allow children to gain confidence through climbing and may even provide a playhouse later on.

• Pretending involves acting out fantasies and playing roles.

Be imaginative with disused items around the house — often the simplest things are the most fun!

Things to Do

Children can find plenty of things to plant and grow. Plant a few cloves of garlic, pointed end up, about 2.5 centimetres deep in a pot (not too close together). After a couple of weeks, long narrow leaves pop up, which may be snipped and used in sandwiches and in salads.

Simple structures made of logs and cloth can be used for imaginative play and can easily become a castle, a tower, a western ranch or a pirate's cave.

• As well as running, jumping and climbing, physical activity can be incorporated into structured play. For instance, two old tyres can provide hours of fun. Children can hide inside them, roll along in them, play tug of war with one, or stand on top of them and attempt to topple each other.

• Adventure playgrounds are enormously popular with children. Some include old cars, bits of scrap, boxes and timber, pieced together in an imaginative way and made safe. Naturally, not

all parents would appreciate having a rusting car hulk in their backyard, however, consider the potential afforded by old wheelbarrows, broken flowerpots, laundry tubs and cracked — not broken — tiles. Naturally, you will need to check that such recycled materials are safe for children. Any protruding bolts or nails should be removed or countersunk into the wood. Steel or wire mesh should be checked for rust and for exposed wire strands; and any pieces of wood should be sound, without any cracks, splinters or signs of excessive wear or rotting. Offcuts of concrete piping and culverts can be used to assemble a wonderful 'adventure playground'. One tip: build a wooden frame around the opening, or glue sections of rubber belting or old tyres to it to avoid heads being bumped on raw concrete.

• Ladders and climbing frames can be a space-efficient inclusion in a play area. As a bonus, the part underneath can double as a private play area or a 'dressing room' for an actor about to play on the lawn 'stage'. To prevent a ladder or climbing frame from becoming slippery when wet, cut notches in the uprights, which will allow water to run off.

• A pair or trio of ropes strung between trees (ensure that it is not too high off the ground) or between a tree and a fence will make a wonderful wobbly climbing frame. A hammock is also great fun strung between two trees. Be careful not to ringbark the trees.

Never forget that, through a child's eyes, the most unlikely aspect of your garden may be the one which they find most appealing. I once watched our little boy tracing the pattern of the bark on a tree for nearly half an hour. Consider the potential of a drain full of rustling leaves and brown water for sailing boats; finding rainbows (beanbows, my son Edward calls them) in the sprinkler; spider-webby compost heaps and stones with earwigs underneath; or even just lying flat on the lawn and gazing at the fluffy clouds drifting overhead.

Trampolines

Trampolining has developed into a highly competitive sport in many parts of the world. Trampolines have been installed in schools and universities and military service training establishments; in fact, American air crews use trampolines as part of their training. Even simple bouncing teaches a child coordination, balance and control, while more complicated exercises, such as somersaults, will enhance any fitness and weight-training program. Even if your children have no intention of pursuing it at an international level, a trampoline in the backyard will provide many happy hours of fun-filled exercise.

Trampolines may be purchased at department stores, sporting goods stores or good toy shops. They vary from a solid sheet of nylon webbing to a type of thin plastic string mesh. Usually, the finer the mesh, the higher the child is able to bounce, depending upon his or her age and experience, of course. If children are to be the main users, and they are new to trampolining, try to find a model that has foam rubber frame pads and clips which fit them to the frame, providing that extra bit of protection should someone thud into the frame. Trampolines provide terrific fun, but, for some reason, they do encourage children to act the fool to the

As long as safety precautions are observed, a trampoline will provide endless fun

delight of an audience. Horseplay of any kind must be checked immediately by a responsible adult, so, before a trampoline is unpacked and set up in the family garden, it is worth noting the following safety precautions when choosing a site for it. Do try to follow them all because safe bouncing is enjoyable bouncing, making for a family garden filled with laughter.

• Make sure there is sufficient space overhead. The ideal spot for a trampoline is in the middle of an open space in the garden, well away from any trees or overhanging branches.

• Keep the area beneath the trampoline absolutely free from any obstruction. Toys, steps, boxes and bicycles are sometimes stored under a trampoline with devastating results for the bouncer. Similarly, anything falling from a bouncing child's pockets, or a ball or toy rolling under the trampoline while it is in use, must be left until the bouncer has stopped and alighted from the trampoline. To crawl under a trampoline to collect something can be very dangerous, both to the bouncer and the retriever.

• Before children play on the trampoline they should be checked for appropriate dress. This only takes a minute and, once again, a little commonsense goes a long way. For beginners, a long-sleeved jumper or sweatshirt and jeans or tracksuit pants are best, weather permitting, as these will minimise any grazes or bruising on knees or elbows. Even in warm weather, thin cotton trousers and big t-shirts, preferably tucked in, should be worn.

• Children should be encouraged to take off their shoes. Gymboots must definitely be discouraged during bouncing. Since the ankle

joint cannot be fully extended while a child is wearing a gymboot, the bouncer can pitch forward onto his or her face, or even onto the trampoline frame. If children's bare feet become sore or grazed, then socks or soft gymnastic shoes should be worn to protect the feet.

• Other articles that should not be worn while trampolining are necklaces, rings, watches, brooches or badges. The decision regarding glasses must be left to the discretion of the child and/or the parent. Naturally it is better if they can be taken off during bouncing, but if the child simply cannot see without them, then it is possible to tie brightly coloured rubber or stretch elastic bands to the ear pieces, which fit snugly around the head, gripping the glasses firmly in place. A long plait or ponytail is best tucked into a shirt collar.

• Children's finger- and toenails will usually be quite short, but it is worth checking that there are no snags which can catch on the webbing.

• Professional trampoline artists employ people called 'spotters', who stand around the edge of the frame. Their job is to continually watch the person bouncing and be prepared to prevent him or her from falling off or being hurt. It is a good safety tip to copy; always try to have someone who is 'out' and, while waiting his or her turn, makes sure that the bouncing is safe.

• Never allow children to eat or drink while bouncing on the trampoline.

• Teach children not to jump straight from the trampoline to the ground. Having been accustomed to the soft, springy landing on the trampoline, a heavy landing on solid ground could injure the feet, knees or spine.

Things to Do

Although growing a tree is regarded by most gardeners as a long-term project, a child will be intrigued to see how quickly a fruit pip or seed will produce a miniature tree. Orange, lemon and grapefruit seeds may all be used; plant about 2 centimetres deep in a pot filled with soil and good quality potting mix.

Treehouses

Did you have a treehouse when you were growing up? Would you like to build such a retreat even now? I suspect that treehouses have been popular with children long before J. M. Barrie immortalised them in *Peter Pan*: 'I shall live with Tink,' said he, 'in a little house we built for Wendy. The fairies are fishing it high up beside their nests in the treetops.'

By building a treehouse, you will be sharing the secret escape used by many famous people, as well as generations of children. Tarzan of the Apes and Winnie the Pooh are both remembered for occupying treehouses, as were Robin Hood and the Swiss Family Robinson. But did you also know that Winston Churchill built a treehouse for his children, and that Queen Victoria used to sketch in an exquisite treehouse at Pitchford, which is now an architectural listed building? Treehouses or 'crow's nests' as they were sometimes called, were a feature of some gardens as early as the 16th century. One that existed in a lime tree for many years at Cobham in England was so large it went for three storeys! Queen Elizabeth I was said to have banqueted among the branches. Treehouses were popular retreats for ladies to work at their embroidery and to gossip and, of course, for children who, with a pocketful of apples, would daydream the summer hours away.

Perhaps the most enjoyable aspect of treehouses is that they are so individual and sentimentally appealing. Whether you aim for one of the elegant, roofed treehouses of

This is a rather grand treehouse; a treehouse made from leftover building materials will be appreciated just as much

yesteryear or simply hammer together a playhouse from fruit box planks in a low-branched tree, a treehouse is enchanting for young and old, a place for quiet play, thinking or reading, far from prying eyes. Tigger Wise says in *Gardens for Children*, 'Any treehouse is better than no treehouse. Even a single board across a low fork fits the fond description, "my treehouse".'

If you are lucky enough to have a variety of trees to choose from, select one with low, spreading boughs, as this will be easiest to reach for securing a flat, firm and steady platform or floor. A mature solid-spreading oak or gum is

Oak trees (Quercus spp.) are very hardy and will support a swing or treehouse

probably the best choice of tree. Avoid trees such as horse chestnuts or crepe myrtles as their limbs tend to snap off under pressure and, naturally, give poisonous shrubs and trees like oleanders a wide berth. An invariable point of compromise is going to be the lopping of branches which get in the way of walls and roof supports or beams. Another option is to build a tree platform within a copse of similar trees, such as pines or spruces, by careful thinning to leave a number of good upright poles, and building in and around the trees and poles.

A treehouse built in a tree that is too young will be pulled apart as the tree grows, even though it may have been well built in the first place. Only build treehouses in mature trees and check them often for signs of wear. The following species have very hard timber and are therefore the most suitable for either attaching a swing or assembling a treehouse: gum trees (*Eucalyptus* spp.), lilly pillies (*Eugenia* and *Syzygium* spp.), oaks (*Quercus* spp.) and ashes (*Fraxinus*), the last three being very hardy. Pine trees are suitable both for climbing and for attaching tree accessories, however, sap running from the tree and getting onto hair and clothes can present a problem.

Another method is to build between the two shady trees, first nailing two pieces of timber between them to make a crossbeam and then lifting a pre-built platform onto the crossbeam and nailing it, securing it at the corners of the two trunks with angled braces. If you elect to build your own treehouse between two trees, you may wish to check with a tree surgeon as to whether they need reinforcing or stabilising before you begin. This can usually be done quite simply by running an insulated cable or padded adjustable turnbuckle between the pair or pairs of trees in question.

Things to Do

A very simple children's water garden may be made from a shallow aluminium foil tray or an old plastic ice cream container. Sink the container into the ground and plant around the rim with creeping ground covers and tiny bulbs, like narcissi.

Try to keep the tree or trees pretty to look at from the outside and from below, and thin the inner branches to make way for the treehouse. This plan offers the additional advantages of shade and privacy for the treehouse inhabitants.

The higher the treehouse, the more sway there will be. Build fairly close to ground level and provide easy access, whether it is a rope ladder or even a fireman's pole. For preference, nail or hinge the ladder to the platform, not to the tree trunk. Nails simply tacked into the tree's trunk are not dependable over time. If young children are likely to be scrambling up and down the ladder, it is a good idea to improve the grip by stretching non-stick tape around the steps, notching them, or winding wire around each step.

The frame of the treehouse platform should be of strong, sturdy, seasoned wood that will not warp. If possible, leave poles and planks out for several months so they are fully seasoned. There are various ways to attach the outer frame of the platform to the tree and/or to any additional pole supports. The easiest treehouse to build is a triangular platform that is secured to the trunk and to two limbs of the tree, resting like a raft on any remaining spreading branches. Nail the frame with galvanised nails. They should not hurt a healthy tree if they are driven in during spring when the sap is running. Try to avoid binding live boughs with ropes or wire as these cut into the tree, weakening it or providing an entry for disease. They are also very difficult to loosen later and can bury themselves in the bark, causing the eventual death of the tree. The bigger the platform, the more space there will be on which to manoeuvre when building a playhouse or attaching the roof; it will also provide more playing area.

Once the frame is in place, nail support

Children need to feel that they have their own space as much as adults do, and what better place than a treehouse?

The treehouse or tree platform may be left open to the sun and moon or you may elect to build a roof. This may be done by carefully securing posts to each corner of the platform and then making a frame between them. There are many choices of roofing material available. Shadecloth is not necessarily weatherproof but is certainly an inexpensive and quite attractive alternative or, if size permits, you can use sheets or hardboard or plywood and cover them with thatching or purchased shingles, nailed down with rust-proof tacks.

For those with their hearts set on a palace in the treetops, walls made from hardboard or plywood can be nailed to each of the corner posts and allowance can be made for inserting windows, made from sheets of perspex, and an old cut-down door. And, if the treehouse is going to be a den for the kids, how about a telephone made from a piece of string, a bell and an old tin can, just for fun, so they can 'call' the main house?

A final tip: as with all garden structures, such as sheds and gazebos, it is wise

beams to it at intervals, then nail one of the flooring planks over this, making sure the boards are level; follow with the rest of the flooring planks. For extra strength, position brackets or angled joists between one platform and the supporting branches or poles and also add walls or some sort of railing at least 1 metre high all around the platform.

to seek your local council's permission for even the simplest treehouse, just on the off-chance that it may end up overhanging a corner of next door's garden, where the neighbour does not appreciate the sounds of children's mirth. This may not necessitate a formal building application, just a letter of intent for approval, but it is wise to check.

Playhouses

Just as it is wise for children and adults to have their own space for private play or thought within the family home, so too do children appreciate getting away from it all in the garden. Children need territories and secret places, and they love to hide — perhaps under

A very simple, pre-fabricated playhouse

A playhouse made from treated pine logs

the verandah or in some dark and weedy cubby hole down at the back fence. Best of all is their very own playhouse.

Some of the best-loved playhouses are the simplest ones, made by children themselves from sticks and bits of cardboard. Even when there is no garden to play in — or if it is too wet — children will improvise a playhouse by throwing a blanket over an arrangement of chairs or by taping a sheet to the side of a stairway. The cardboard box in which a new fridge or washing machine is delivered can make a good playhouse, too. Unfortunately, while these 'playhouses' provide plenty of fun, they are only temporary and do not provide the basic safety and security offered by a more solid playhouse.

An enthusiastic and capable builder could turn his or her hand to making a playhouse. The lovely thing about a homemade playhouse is that it is unique and can become a family heirloom, with only a fresh coat of paint needed to mark the passing years. Plans are often given in home renovator or builder publications and may be enlarged to scale. It is then a matter of finding the wood and other supplies and commencing building. Remember, when building a playhouse, avoid unsafe materials: sharp, unfinished edges, rough or splintery wood, protruding nails or bolts, poisonous lead-based paints and glass or plastics that shatter. One other tip: if you are unsure of the scale to use, measure the critical dimension for the project — a child's leg, arm and height. Be sure to allow for children's rapid growth.

Alternatively, you can purchase a readymade playhouse. There is an enormous variety available to suit every size of garden and parental wallet. Some of the newer styles are made from treated split pine logs and look like little cabins, with an optional verandah, slide or rope ladder. Some even have window boxes — a must for children who are fascinated with the idea of

Safety Tip

Avoid inhaling smoke from burning plants unless you know exactly what they are, as some give off noxious fumes.

growing their own plants. Purchased playhouses may either be delivered in a prepacked form or assembled in the yard for a small fee.

Before you do either, run a cursory eye over existing structures in the yard. It is quite possible that a disused garden shed or pergola over a driveway could be suitably painted, decorated and furnished for children to use. One of my friends found an old, disused telephone box and restored it, removed the glass and set it up as a doorway to their old tool shed, then painted the whole thing a vivid cherry red. Her son's friends, all avid 'Doctor Who' fans, love to play in the 'Tardis' playhouse.

Whether you elect to build or buy a playhouse, or to adapt an existing structure, the first thing you should do is check the local building regulations. A quick call to the council is usually all that is required and can save a lot of heartache if a playhouse has to be re-sited or, at worst, taken down completely.

There are certain important features you should check when considering a playhouse. Firstly, it must be weatherproof. It should have at least one external door and window, preferably two. There really is no need for the doors and windows to be locked, unless you are concerned about animals camping in there; it is too tempting for children to lock playmates inside for 'a joke'. If the playhouse does have a key, ensure it is kept by an adult, preferably in an out-of-reach cupboard. The windows should be made so that they can be opened to ensure adequate ventilation. When glazing windows, avoid using glass; use instead an impact-resistant plastic material.

If the floor is to be concreted, build the slab on a sand bedding with a plastic water barrier on top of the sand. This will ensure that the floor does not become damp or smelly. It is, however, permanent and if you plan to reclaim that part of the garden at a later date, it is probably better to build or buy a playhouse with a wooden or plywood floor and frame. The floor's supporting structure should be at least 30 centimetres above the ground to allow ventilation and prevent the floorboards from rotting.

For safety's sake, it is important that a playhouse should be a reasonable size. Not too large — commonsense will guide you — but be sure that at least two or three children can sit or sprawl comfortably inside as they will invariably have friends in there, too. It is also important that an adult be able to enter freely, if not necessarily stand upright, for several reasons. For one, there may be an accident; more prosaically, the playhouse will need regular cleaning or at least hosing out, and inspections for pests and insects are also advisable. Ants, in particular, will swarm in during the warmer weather to polish

off any biscuit crumbs left behind. Of course, from the child's point of view, these cleaning-up sessions should be kept to a minimum. After all, bedrooms have to be cleaned but kids do not care if a playhouse is grubby or messy — that is just the way they like it!

As far as furnishing the playhouse, very little is really needed. Traditional favourites include old packing crates (sanded thoroughly to minimise splinters) and the old potty chair with the hole filled in. Any old lampshades, plastic bowls, left-over carpet, prints or bits of curtain fabric or linoleum are all assured of a good home if you have a playhouse in the garden. An old disconnected telephone is a real treasure. And, for the traditional 'sleep-outside' night, usually with at least one friend, a sleeping bag and a midnight snack are all that is required.

Special Trees

The majority of adults will be very aware of the importance of trees to the world's ecosystem, not to mention their foliage and flower potential in the family garden. Trees also provide privacy from neighbours and much-needed shade in summer. Most family gardens do not provide the space to grow very large trees, like Moreton Bay figs, for instance. Enjoy these in a nearby park, instead. Trees for the family garden may be selected for autumn foliage, such as the Japanese maple or the Chinese tallow tree (*Sapium sebiferum*). Springtime is blossom time and you can give the feeling of the seasons to your family's garden by planting one of the flowering fruit trees, such as peach or apple. Fruit trees, of course, present a wonderful bonus to children — they can eat while they climb! *Prunus* trees produce lovely blossom in spring and they are also a good tree for small children to climb and play in. Some handsome garden trees also feature quite beautiful bark on their trunks, such as crepe myrtle (*Lagerstroemia indica*) and several of the Australian native gum

trees, such as the bloodwood (*Eucalyptus gummifera*). If you have a crepe myrtle, take the children out in the garden after it has rained and show them the interesting and decorative patterns that form on the rich, tawny-striped trunk.

From a child's point of view, the best sort of tree in the family garden is one that can be climbed. Trees also provide a great place to hang a swing (see pages 101–3) and are, naturally, excellent places to build a treehouse (see pages 107–10). Not all trees are suitable, though. Ideally, a 'special tree' for children to play in should have a short trunk, low sturdy branches, smooth, non-scratchy bark and should not have poisonous or potentially irritating sap, leaves, nuts, fruit or flowers. Consider the following: peppercorn tree (*Schinus molle*), jacaranda (*Jacaranda mimosifolia*) and horse chestnut (*Aesculus hippocastanum*). A Japanese maple (*Acer palmatum*) is very suitable for a small garden as it rarely grows taller than 6 metres. It provides a lovely cool dappled green retreat for a child in summer, though I think this tree is probably at its loveliest in autumn, when the leaves turn fiery orange, red and yellow by turns. As with all autumn foliage trees, a Japanese maple should be planted in full sun; the more sun, the more colour it will produce.

In a large garden, you could plant either a liquidambar (*Liquidambar styraciflua*) or a camphor laurel (*Cinnamomum camphora*) but be warned, they will grow to between 15 and 20 metres, at least. We had a liquidambar when I was growing up and I used to often climb it with my friend from next door. I loved the star-shaped gold and purple leaves in autumn and used to collect the prickly seed pods and spray paint them gold and silver. However, whenever I visit my mother's house now, she grimly points to those same seed pods clogging up the gutters and to the tree's massive roots buckling the fence. Like all elements in the family garden, a compromise will have to be reached when it comes to trees. Ideally, a very large tree should

*The glorious autumn tones of the Japanese maple (*Acer palmatum*)*

be planted in the centre of the lawn; if necessary, in later years, you can design and build an entertaining area or patio around it.

We have a lilly pilly (*Syzygium luehmannii*) in our garden which is quite climbable and produces nice, bright pink edible berries that can be made into jam. Be careful when buying lilly pilly as some varieties can grow into towering trees 30 metres tall!

A magnolia is possibly the most elegant of all the flowering trees with its dark green leaves and wonderful, fragrant flowers. Look for *Magnolia stellata* (small white starry flowers), *M. grandiflora* (an evergreen with richly perfumed white flowers) or the ever-popular *M. soulangiana* (deep pink/pink flowers). Magnolias should not be placed in a narrow garden bed, as their branches need room to fork low and spread wide. The only disadvantage with magnolia is that, unlike the other trees mentioned here, they are very slow-growing and your children will be bringing their own children to visit you before your tree is ready to be climbed!

Some trees are loved by children even if they are not really easy to climb. When I was about ten years old, one of my friends had a weeping willow tree at the bottom of her garden and we all loved to hide behind its long green curtains of branches to play and peek out. Pine trees provide wonderful toys in the form of squishy, sharp-scented needles and cones to collect. Casuarina trees have fascinated children for generations — you pull the needles apart

and then stick them back together again . . . remember? Trees like scribbly gum (*Eucalyptus haemastoma*) will be appealing to children because of their bark, as will paperbarks (*Melaleuca quinquenervia*) and pussywillow's (*Salix caprea*) catkins will prove irresistible.

When attaching anything to trees, like steps or ropes, always remember that the tree is alive. A rope tied around a branch will eventually ringbark it. So, if you want to hang a swing, it is actually better for the tree to bolt it into place (see page 102) and reduce the likelihood of introducing infection. Ropes may be hung from branches for temporary play but they should not encircle the branch too tightly. A good tip is to cushion the rope with a piece of rubber strapping — conveyor belting is very good for this, as are sections of old hoses.

Never contemplate using any of the following as potential 'special trees' for children: birch (*Betula*), beech (*Fagus*), cypress (*Cupressus*), poplar (*Populus*) or elm (*Ulmus*). All are quite brittle-timbered and susceptible to wood rots. Other unsuitable choices include holly (*Ilex*) with its prickly leaves and poisonous berries and oleander, all parts of which are poisonous. To double-check whether a tree's sap, leaves, flowers or fruit may be dangerous to children, refer to Poisonous Plants on page 169–72.

Just as you would check any other item of outdoor equipment, check children's special trees regularly to maintain maximum safety. Early leaf fall or late flowering indicate poor health in the

Things to Do

Show children how to take cuttings from easy-to-grow geraniums, coleus or Busy Lizzies (*Impatiens*), removing lower leaves from the stem before planting and leaving at least two pairs of leaves on top. Explain that it is best to nip off any flowers as these may drain energy that the cutting needs to produce roots and become a new plant. Set aside a shelf, window sill or low table where children can look after their motley collection of cuttings in various stages of growth — and decrepitude.

stems, trunk or roots. Even sick-looking buds can indicate a problem. Signs to look for include:

- Trunk damage — any wood rot, splitting or dieback can be a real safety hazard.

- Twig die back (root or soil problems).

- Branches falling — with most trees, some lower branches will die naturally as new ones develop and shade the older branches. Check lower climbing branches regularly and remove them if weak, nailing steps to the trunk, if necessary.

Outdoor Toys

Ideas for outdoor toys in the family garden include slides, seesaws, rope ladders, tepees and go-karts or billycarts. Most are readily available from department stores or specialised suppliers. Generally, they are also quite easy to make and will provide children with many hours of enjoyment. Other traditional favourites for outdoor play include a hobby horse, a wheelbarrow and kites (see page 122).

ROPE LADDERS

Take a length of thick rope; the amount needed depends on the number of rungs and knots you plan to have. You will need 15-millimetre thick hardboard planks, approximately 335 x 80 millimetres plus two 60-millimetre carbine clips (from boating supply shops). Drill holes for the rope 25 millimetres in from each end of each rung. Cut the rope in half and tie a knot to form a small loop on the end of each piece of rope. Put a clip on each loop, sling the loops over a suitably strong living tree branch and snap the clips over the ropes underneath. Tie a loose knot in each double length, slide it up to the clips and pull tight. Then fit the rungs by first tying knots at the same height, then threading on a rung and tying a double knot beneath each one. Proceed with tying on rungs, spacing them about 250 millimetres apart. If desired, secure loose ends of rope ladder into ground with tent pegs.

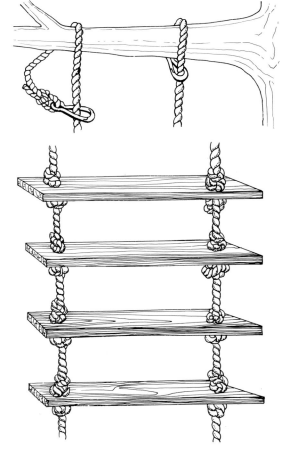

1. Tie a loop in the end of each rope and attach a carbine clip. Put the ropes over a tree branch and fasten the clips over the rope underneath; tie a knot under the clips.
2. Tie a knot in the rope, slide a rung up to the knot and tie a double knot underneath. Continue this way until the ladder is the desired length.

GO-KARTS OR BILLYCARTS

Go-karts must be sturdy and easy to steer and brake. They are usually made very simply with a fixed rear axle and a pivoting front axle, joined together by a frame which provides seating for the child driver. Steering can be controlled by foot ropes in more sophisticated models or just by hand ropes, in much the same way as reins are used to guide a horse. It is actually safest to use both methods together, as this makes the kart easier to control. The frame should be made from wood and bolted — not nailed — together. Nails will always work loose and scratch the rider. If you are going to varnish or paint the kart, do so as you go along, but leave free any areas that are to be glued.

Axles may be made of steel or wood. Traditional 'made-by-grandpa' go-karts usually have wooden axles that may be more easily fitted to take that noisy favourite wheel

substitute, the ball bearing. Old ball bearings can be obtained from service stations or car detailing workshops that work on heavy gearboxes. Rubber-tyred wheels, such as those used for lawn mowers or prams, are a quieter but slightly more expensive option.

TEPEES

Children will love having a powwow in a colourful backyard tepee. Tepees were the traditional homes of Native American tribes, such as the Sioux. They were usually made from tanned bison hide and were painted with symbols representing natural power, the hunt and war. Zigzags, for instance, meant lightning and unbroken circles represented the unity of the world.

To put up a tepee frame, you will need eight 2.1-metre bamboo poles, 91 centimetres of strong cord and some tent pegs or skewers. The tepee cover can be made from five pieces of unbleached calico, each 180 centimetres long, cut into a triangular shape with a curved base measuring 115 centimetres. Print or applique appropriate symbols on these pieces, then stitch them together in a semicircle, double hemming all edgings and securing the hole at the top with bias binding. Sew eight to ten 15-centimetre lengths of tape at equal intervals along the long straight edge — these will be the ties used to close the tepee flap. Sew peg loops to the curved base, say three to each of the four panels, leaving the fifth one, the flap, to hang free.

Children love to get dirty — a dirt heap in the garden will keep them amused for hours

To assemble, lash three poles together in a tripod. (*Note:* a purchased tepee has poles which are usually notched or have holes drilled in their ends to facilitate lashing, so you could try this to make things more secure.) Then lash the remaining five poles to the tripod at equal points around the circle. Drop the cover over the frame, tying three tapes together at the top and pulling the base loops down to be pegged out evenly into the ground. Open the tent flap and tie it back.

If you are out of ideas or money for entertaining children in the family garden, consider the following suggestions for outdoor toys and games:

• Make a simple sundial. Ask an adult to set up a post or broom handle in the middle of the yard and then collect together 12 'time markers', which can be chunks of timber or clean, empty yoghurt tubs. On each one, write a time: 6 A.M., 7 A.M., 8 A.M., right through to 5 P.M. Now, all you need to do is check your watch every hour and run out to push in a time marker where the post's shadow has moved. It is fun to check in a day or two and see the difference in the shadows caused by the daily changes of the movement of the earth around the sun.

• Set aside a corner of the garden for a dirt heap. (For the fastidious parent, remember that your carpets

Nature-watching in the garden is fun

Things to Do

School holidays are a good time to give children a gardening project. They like to build things, so what about a rock garden? This can be part of the main garden's rockery feature (see pages 75–7) or a smaller, less elaborate feature. Collect together some leftover pieces of landscaping rock, pack them together with soil and plant the cracks with small succulents, herbs, bulbs or tufty grasses.

and walls are going to be ruined anyway, so why fuss?) Get kids to change into old clothes first. Pile up soil in a shaded spot and they can run riot, making tunnels, castles, roads and cities. As a bonus, there will always be plenty of soil on hand for flower beds.

• Send children on safari around the garden. Teach them to look carefully amongst the leaf litter for 'wildlife', such as caterpillars, ants and millipedes. If you have a plastic bug-catcher, so much the better, otherwise an old glass jar will do for picking up any particularly interesting bug to look at. Encourage children to wear gardening gloves for this game, just to be on the safe side.

Parties and Games

Whatever the size, shape or condition of your lawn, your family can use every inch of it for outdoor recreation. There is a wide variety of games and sports suitable for all seasons and for players of all ages. You could go in for traditional sports like badminton, or perhaps you could try something quite different, like archery. Children aged seven years and up will enjoy activities like horseshoe pitching; teenagers can entertain friends with a vigorous game of volleyball and putting a golf ball provides a more leisurely game for all. Make the most of your garden with a selection of games.

ARCHERY AND DARTS

Bows and arrows date back to the days of cavemen, when they were instruments of survival rather than of sport. Even in medieval times archery was enjoyed as a sport. Under the patronage of Charles II, nobles and commoners alike took great pleasure in demonstrating their skill at outdoor archery tournaments.

Archery equipment is simple and usually relatively inexpensive. A good junior set will comprise a bow, several arrows, a quiver and a target. For archers who wish to take their game more seriously, say, in school competitions, arm guards and finger guards or gloves may also be necessary.

Driveways provide a nice safe area for archery practice. A piece of corkboard or balsa can be tacked onto the garage door if you are shooting suction cap arrows, to avoid cupping-marks. If you are shooting arrows from a purchased archery set, you can either secure the target onto the same protective board, or make an extra backstop of bags of dried grass and secure the target over this.

Darts can also give a lot of pleasure. Dartboards are usually made from soft wood or cork and the players' darts come in sets of three.

Unlike archery, darts has the advantage of being able to be played inside a garage or cellar if outdoor games are rained out for the day.

Remember that both archery and darts are potentially dangerous games and safety precautions should be exercised. Children should be supervised by a responsible adult.

BADMINTON

Army officers are credited with bringing this game to England where it was first played at Badminton in Avon, from which the game takes its name.

Originally a woollen ball was used as the shuttlecock, then cork, feathers and finally specially designed and weighted nylon 'birds' were developed. It is the design of the shuttlecock that gives the game its unique appeal and makes it especially suitable for a small garden. With a gentle hit, the shuttlecock floats; with a hard one, it can travel at a fast pace, but not too far. Plastic shuttlecocks are, on average, a little heavier than the cork and feather type, making them more suitable for outdoor play. They also wear better.

When selecting badminton racquets, look for ones which are fairly flexible in the shaft. It is the player's fingers and wrist which control the movement of the racquet, unlike tennis, for example, even though the forehand and backhand grips are similar.

Steel-stringed racquets cost more than nylon-stringed ones, but are much more durable. Similarly, wood- or nylon-shafted racquets are extremely light and relatively inexpensive, but it is the steel or hardened aluminium varieties that will have the longest life. A badminton kit will include four racquets, a net and supports, and at least one shuttlecock, along with a pamphlet of rules and instructions. Badminton can be played on any flat, level surface; just mark out the court area with chalk or tape, according to instructions.

And, for a fun game on a hot summer's day, how about a game of 'balloonminton'? Instead of using shuttlecocks, blow up several small balloons. You can weight them with a teaspoon or so of water, thereby adding an element of fun and risk to a hard hit!

BASKETBALL PRACTICE

With the wide popularity of basketball, no family garden is complete without an all-weather net, a wooden or fibreglass backboard and a hoop or ring.

The best spot for mounting it is usually the garage, allowing plenty of concrete or a paved area for dribbling or feinting practice and,

Things to Do

Plant a young tree for each of your children. Make a note of the tree's 'birthday' and, each year, take a photo of each child next to his or her tree.

hopefully, it should not be too close to glass windows or doors. The hoop is usually positioned 3 metres from the ground. However, if you have very small children, you might consider bending the regulations and moving it closer to their height. Ensure that the hoop is securely fixed to the wall or stand. Mark throwing lines on the driveway with chalk and use them for easy contests.

Consider these variations on the simple throw:

• Throwing the ball sideways with one arm

• Holding both hands over the head and throwing the ball from this position

• Facing away from the hoop and throwing the ball backwards

CROQUET

This is derived from *pall-mall*, a game that spread from France to England and became a popular sport for gentlemen in the 17th century. In the original game, a mallet was used to drive a ball along an alley and through a ring. It is the reason London's Pall Mall was so named; it was once a well-known venue for the game.

The roles for croquet have not really changed very much since those days and it remains a game that can be enjoyed by young and old. A croquet set comprises hard wooden balls, each painted a different colour, plus mallets, wickets and stakes that mark out the course between the wickets. Ideally, a lawn for croquet should be about 30 metres long, however, it is perfectly possible to play it on a much smaller one. The object of the game is to hit the balls through the wickets in a certain order — and this is harder than it sounds, particularly when you have to turn around! The first player (or team) to go through the whole course and hit the home stake wins.

Children love to make things 'fly'

FRISBEES AND KITES

A rather dubious story of Elihu Frisbee, a Yale College student in 1827, who rebelled against compulsory chapel attendance by throwing the collection plate across the campus grounds, has been handed down to explain the origin of this game of flying discs. Frisbees come in a wide variety of colours and sizes — some even glow in the dark — and they are a very inexpensive means of ensuring some exhilarating play for all the family. The most common forms of frisbee-tossing are the underhand delivery and the backhand throw; both are basically wrist-action movements.

Provided you have a reasonable amount of free air space in your garden and you are not hemmed in by powerlines or thick trees, a soaring kite can be fun. For young children, coloured streamers tied to a hoop made from an old plastic ice cream container lid will give just as much fun.

Making a kite is a simple project. The most common variety is a simple flat kite, made from two crossed sticks, each about 1 metre long, a sheet of plastic or nylon cloth, and a tail, all held together with sticky tape and glue. Make holes at each end of the sticks and in the middle of one, and about 45 centimetres from the top of the

other. Place them together over the holes and securely tie together. Thread a string between the other four holes and cover the cross-like grid with the cloth, gluing and/or stapling around the string; be sure the cloth is smooth and very taut. Of course, commercially made kites are readily available and they are very quick to assemble. Tie string across both sticks between holes and then tie the long kite-flying string to the central cross, approximately one-third from the top point; this should result in correct balance. Now, put your back to the wind, toss the kite up and let out some line!

HORSESHOE PITCHING

This is a terrific game for the smallest garden or even a courtyard. It is not a strenuous game, rather it is one of skill, making it fun for people of varying ages and levels of accuracy. Horseshoe pitching sets, comprising four or six metal horseshoes and two stakes (either embedded in a weight or to be driven into the ground) are generally available from toy and hobby stores. Some are even made from heavy plastic or rubber, but the purists will argue that they lack the satisfying 'clunk' of metal on metal.

VOLLEYBALL

The game of volleyball was first demonstrated at an American YMCA conference in 1896. The first ball was actually the inner lining of a basketball, for no other ball available at the time was light enough. Volleyball is a sport that boasts many enthusiasts and is a fairly recent addition to the list of Olympic sports. The variation of beach volleyball has also attracted considerable attention.

While an official court needs to be 18 metres long, the game may be adapted to a smaller space. Similarly, while the official net height is up to 2.7 metres, it can be lowered to allow younger children to join in. Volleyball can be played with up to nine players per team, or with as few as two players per team. Volleyball game

Blowing bubbles is always fun, and the garden is the perfect place

sets should include the net and net supports, plus an inflatable ball and booklet of game rules. *Note:* It is important to use only a proper volleyball for this game. A ball that is too heavy or too hard can hurt hands and wrists and one that is too light will burst during strenuous play.

Some more old-fashioned favourites for good times in the backyard will include:

- Beanbag tossing
- Handball (against a brick wall or garage door)
- Hopscotch
- Skipping
- Marble games
- Blowing bubbles
- A pogo stick race or stilts
- Hula hoops

Games that are especially suitable for children's parties include:

- Passing oranges under the chin
- Musical chairs
- Obstacle races
- Tunnel ball
- Balloon- or egg-passing races
- 'Simon Says' or 'Follow the Leader'
- Tug-of-war
- Three-legged races
- Relays
- Treasure hunt
- Sack races and wheelbarrow races

SKIPPING ROPE GAMES

Children like to recite rhymes while they are jumping a skipping rope. This is just one of many skipping rhymes which have been passed down from one generation to another.

> Cinderella, dressed in yellow,
> Went upstairs to kiss her fellow,
> How many kisses did she get?
> One . . . two . . . three . . . four . . . five . . .
>   six (turn faster)

> Cinderella, dressed in blue
> Went upstairs to shine her shoes,
> How many shoes did she shine?
> One . . . two . . . three . . . four . . . five . . .
>   six (turn faster)

> Cinderella, dressed in green,
> Went upstairs to sleep and dream,
> How many dreams did she have?
> One . . . two . . . three . . . four . . . five . . .
>   six (turn faster)

> Cinderella, dressed in pink,
> Went upstairs to get some ink,
> How many letters did she write?
> One . . . two . . . three . . . four . . . five . . .
>   six (turn faster)

> Cinderella, dressed in brown,
> Went upstairs to make a gown,
> How many gowns did she make?
> One . . . two . . . three . . . four . . . five . . .
>   six (turn faster)

Finally, if you are planning to enjoy plenty of family fun and games in your garden, consider making or buying a storage box or cupboard for the equipment. Set it up in the laundry or garage; this way, sets of larger items like croquet mallets and badminton racquets are not broken up and lost.

4

CRAFTY NATURE IDEAS FOR CHILDREN

Miniature Gardens

Some suburban gardening clubs run competitions for 'gardens in a seed tray'. What is usually required is a garden scene in miniature, including as many realistic features as possible, such as lawn, paths, fences, borders and perhaps even a fish pond. (Older children could use a mirror for this, while younger ones could smooth out a piece of shiny aluminium foil.)

It may be necessary for an adult to discuss things with the child initially, making suggestions and putting forward ideas, but the end result should be the youngster's own work. This is another great project for a child who is ill and housebound or for one who lives in an apartment, as they can landscape 'their' own garden without having to go outside. Miniature gardens can become an absorbing indoor hobby. They can be made with cacti or other easy-care plants, like petunias, miniature geraniums, lobelias, sweet alyssum, stock, pansies, violas and dwarf French marigolds. Little spring-flowering bulbs, like grape hyacinths, are also nice in a miniature garden.

Show children that the garden can be a source of materials for a range of craft projects

You can now fill in the spaces with the plants or cuttings. For a very small garden, an ordinary tablespoon is a better planting tool than a garden trowel. Dig up some small mosses or ferns and grasses from the garden and plant them in a partly shaded miniature garden. Be sure to keep them moist and reasonably well spaced. A cacti garden, on the other hand, should be sited in full sun. With cacti, teach children to wear gloves (preferably heavy duty rubber or canvas) when handling them. Gently squeeze pots so the roots come out with the earth around them before popping them into place in the garden; press down the soil and water in well. For some children, just as much enjoyment will be gained from the non-planting part. They may even prefer to stock their garden with dry twigs, leaves and picked flowers, changing the arrangement every day. Older children tend to have a bit more patience and will wait for the seeds to appear.

You will need plants or seeds, foil or a small mirror, pebbles, gravel and small pretty rocks, extra plant pots or saucers, potting mix, compost and a suitable container. This can be as simple and inexpensive as an old ice cream container, or you could buy an attractive shallow terracotta bowl. We have a pair of old laundry tubs we have used — one is a water garden and the other a miniature garden, filled with aluminium plant, maidenhair fern, small-leafed ivy and violas. A waterproofed wooden crate would also be a suitable container for a miniature garden.

Half-fill the container with gravel, then finish filling with potting mix and compost; leaf mould is particularly good. Lay the piece of foil or mirror to be used as a fish pond on the soil. You can place extra plant pots or saucers, upended, in the soil as you go to create mountains and hills as a backdrop to the garden. Make roads, walls and bridges from the pebbles and small rocks. Hobby shops and garden suppliers have a wonderful array of tiny figures, animals and Japanese-style temples that can be very tempting.

Tip

It is quite easy for a child to make a pretty and unusual garden by growing the tops of root vegetables. Cut the top off a carrot, turnip or parsnip, leaving 0.5 centimetres of the root and 0.5 centimetres of the leaf stem. Put a layer of pebbles or stones on the bottom of a shallow bowl and then stand the root tops — leaf stumps uppermost — on top and leave on a sunny window sill to drink. A pineapple top may also sprout when handled in the same way.

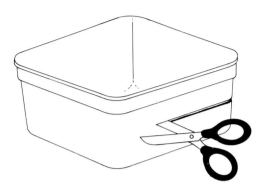

1. Cut down a plastic ice cream or similar container to form the base of the garden.

2. Fill the container with soil; you can use small pots to contain some plants.

3. 'Landscape' the garden with rocks, pebbles and any other decorative features.

4. Lastly, add the plants, arranging the taller or larger ones to the back and smaller ones to the front.

Bonsai, the art of growing miniature trees, may appeal to some children. The great advantage of bonsai trees is that they do not take up much room. Pine, larch, maple or weeping willow all make good subjects. In spring, take a cutting from the parent tree, using a vigorous-looking side shoot, about 50 centimetres long. Plant the lower third of the cutting in potting mix with starter powder and in a few weeks it should develop roots and start to grow.

The following spring it can be transferred to a shallow container with good drainage. When planting the cutting, place a generous measure of fresh compost around its base. Then, every year, prune the shoots and start to train them to the edge of the pot with string or florist's wire. Every second year, in spring, the bonsai plant will need to be lifted, the roots pruned by about a third and the container filled with fresh compost. It might take a number of years but eventually the miniature tree will take on a gnarled appearance. Study a fully grown tree first and try to get the same effect with the miniature one. You must water your bonsai regularly, never letting the soil dry out. It will grow best outside in a sheltered position. Bonsai is fiddly work and the tree may take years to grow to the shape you desire, but it is a very satisfying and involving hobby.

Bottle Gardens

A garden growing inside a bottle has the same fascination as a ship in a bottle. The concept of bottle gardens resulted from the work of Nathaniel Ward, a 19th-century English doctor. He found that ferns and mosses grew well when protected in glass-sided boxes. Once a bottle garden is established, the plants will grow very well. The plants inside the bottle will be protected from draughts, central heating, smoke and dust, none of which they like. A bottle garden can even be left for several months without watering.

Any small ornamental plants usually grown indoors are suitable for bottle gardens. They need to be reasonably small and slow-growing so that they do not swamp the bottle. It is not easy to prune them if they get too big! Ivies are good, especially the pretty gold variegated 'Buttercup' or 'Goldheart' or the silver 'Glacier'. *Saintpaulia* (African violets) grow particularly well in a bottle garden because they are delicate and need

a warm, damp atmosphere. Ferns are very suitable for bottle gardens; select varieties with contrasting foliage to create an interesting display, for example, *Adiantum* spp., maidenhair (frothy green fronds), *Asplenium nidus* (glossy, dark green, strap-like leaves) and *Davallia bullata* (broad, leathery leaves). Children may like to collect small ferns and mosses from garden walls, paths or nearby bushland, but you will probably have to purchase most plants.

Other specimens suitable for a bottle garden are those that like close, moist conditions. For example, *Peperomia magnoliifolia* (medium green–cream leaves), *Begonia foliosa* (small glossy green and burgundy leaves), *Ficus pumila* (green heart-shaped leaves), *Tradescantia fluminensis* (a trailing plant with small white flowers), and *Zebrina pendula* (grey leaves with a pink or purple central stripe). If you have selected a tall bottle, then *Dracaena sanderana* (grey/ivory leaves) or *Agalaonema commutatum* (green leaves with silvery spots) would add height to your arrangement of plants. Children like unusual plants, like the starfish plant (*Cryptanthus bivittatus*) or the weird blotchy peacock plant (*Maranta* spp.). Mother-in-law's tongue (*Sansevieria*) makes a good spiky centrepiece for a tall bottle.

A desert-style bottle garden is perhaps the easiest to establish because it only needs watering on rare occasions, when a light misting may be all that is required. In a desert-style bottle garden, only tiny cacti or similar succulent plants should be grown. Sand, gravel, pebbles — even a colourful china Mexican figure — could all be used to create a suitable effect.

The main 'ingredients' you will need to make a bottle garden are dexterity and patience. It is a good school holiday project as it demands quite a bit of time. Still, once the garden is made, it needs little attention, apart from removing dead leaves and occasional watering. Bottle gardens are a terrific idea for children who may be housebound through illness, or living in a flat with no access to a garden. They can grow their very own garden in a bottle and learn about nature's cycles as they watch their plants grow and support each other.

Take a large, reasonably flat-based glass bottle, preferably with a wide mouth — a wine flagon or carboy is ideal — or a large biscuit jar or sweets jar on its side. Wash and dry the bottle thoroughly. Line the bottom of the bottle garden with small stones or gravel, then sprinkle with

sand. Using a paper funnel so as not to make a mess around the sides of the bottle, pour in a few inches of light, *dry* sandy soil. It is important that the soil is not wet when it goes into the bottle, as it will clump and stick to the sides of the bottle as it goes down. Mix it with a little dried charcoal if you like; this will help to keep the soil from becoming sour. Clean the sides of the bottle as you go, using a small sponge on a long cane or piece of wire.

1. Using a paper funnel, fill the bottle with a layer of dry, sandy soil.

2. Using a spoon taped to a piece of cane or a skewer, spread the soil evenly around the bottom of the bottle; you can use a fork taped to a cane as a tiny rake.

3. With the help of your tiny gardening implements, arrange the plants in the soil.

4. Tamp down the soil using a cotton reel attached to a piece of cane, then water the bottle garden using a fine spray.

Collect together a selection of tiny plantlets and seedlings (the smaller the better, making it easier to introduce them through the bottle's neck). Alternatively, sprinkle a few seeds into the bottom of the bottle garden and cover with a fine layer of soil. Tape a baby's spoon and fork to thin bamboo canes or skewers and use these to plant the seedlings in the desired arrangement. Use the fork to gently rake soil over the plants' roots wherever possible. Still, even if this is not always possible, the plants will likely re-root quickly in the humidity of the bottle garden.

You could also do what professional florists do when they make a bottle garden and use a 'soil-firmer'. This implement is made by gluing or taping an old cotton reel to a cane or skewer and using it to tamp down the earth around the plants. You can use pincers or tweezers taped to long handles to move plants about, placing the tall ones in the centre or at the back. Bark, twigs and tiny rocks may be used to secure plants in place and also to give a more realistic woodland appearance.

Once planting is complete, water once, using

Things to Do

Many older children show an interest in a particular group of plants — alpines, for instance, or begonias. Some children like to collect cacti and they will flower well on a sunny windowsill. Paying their annual subscription to the appropriate specialist society is a good way to encourage such an interest.

a tube or fine mister. A spray is preferable so you do not splash earth on the leaves, or trickle water carefully down the sides of the bottle. Never over-water a bottle garden as the water will collect and gradually stagnate, poisoning the plants. Then cork or cap the bottle tightly. You will easily be able to tell whether there is too much or too little water in your bottle garden. There should be condensation on the inside of the top third of the bottle. If there is more than this, leave the stopper or lid off for a day or so. If there is less, mist in a little extra water and reseal.

Corking or capping is not always done and bottle gardens are sometimes half-sealed, allowing some air to enter. However, the idea is to create a completely enclosed atmosphere which becomes self-sufficient — moisture that condenses on the leaves ultimately drips off and returns to the roots, keeping the cycle of life going. Keep the bottle garden in a light spot well away from direct sunlight and rotate it regularly.

Growing Bulbs Indoors

Some of the bulbs suitable for growing indoors in pots are crocus, freesias, galanthus, hyacinth, ranunculus, narcissus, anemones, dwarf iris, sparaxis and tulips. (*Note:* the term 'bulb' has been used generally in this chapter to include both bulbs and corms, as well as tuberous-rooted and rhizomatous plants.) Bulbs are easy to grow and some may even be persuaded to flower in midwinter, their clear bright colours marking an

end to cold weather, if they are planted about four months beforehand. 'Hurrying up' bulbs in this way is called 'forcing'.

As long as you buy good, sound bulbs and observe a few simple rules to set the growing process in motion, there's nothing too difficult about growing bulbs indoors. It is best to buy bulbs that have been specially treated by the growers to bloom early. All new bulbs already have the flowers and leaf shoots inside and only

Tip

Children love plants that have unusually textured foliage or flowers. They will be fascinated by the soft down on the leaves of *Salvia argentea* or the velvety finish of *Stachys byzantina* 'Silver Carpet'.

1. Put a layer of compost or special bulb fibre in the bottom of a bowl.

2. Set the bulbs in the bowl.

3. Carefully fill the spaces between the bulbs with compost, pressing it down with your fingers, and moisten the compost. Put the bowls in a cool, dark place for six to eight weeks.

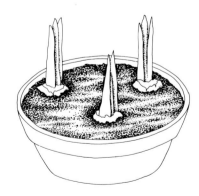

4. When the leaf shoots reach about 10 cm, bring the bowl into a lighted room or onto a window sill.

need a little encouragement to flower completely. Hyacinths can be grown to perfection indoors, provided there's a cool dark place to store them after planting; the same goes for tulips, while grape hyacinths and crocus are most successful under fairly cool indoor conditions. Daffodils are probably the most obliging, growing happily in pots or troughs, either on balconies or inside, without the need of cool, dark conditioning. Most bulbs need to start their growth in the dark. This ensures they will grow good strong roots, so important later when they will feed the leaves and flowers.

You might like to buy a special bulb bowl or planter but any shallow bowl will do for small bulbs. Put a layer of compost or bulb fibre (either purchased from a garden centre or made up yourself, using one part each charcoal, sand and moistened peat moss) in the bottom of the bowl. This will help to anchor the bulb's roots. Clean garden soil can also be added, providing it does not contain fresh organic matter likely to decompose and go sour.

Having bought your bulbs, store them in a light airy place. About four weeks before planting, transfer them to the crisper tray in the refrigerator. Keeping the bulbs cool, moist and in the dark is essential for good root development in container-grown bulbs and for good flowers to follow. Bulbs can be grown indoors without being refrigerated first, but they will usually flower later, closer to their actual time in the garden.

Set the bulbs firmly on the soil or fibre in the bowl, as close as you can. It does not matter if they touch each other. Carefully fill up the spaces between the bulbs with potting mix and compost, firming it down gently between them until the container is almost full. Moisten the compost slightly, but do not soak it. The necks

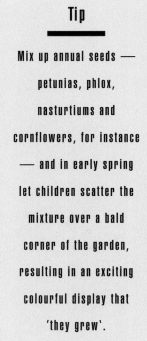

Tip

Mix up annual seeds — petunias, phlox, nasturtiums and cornflowers, for instance — and in early spring let children scatter the mixture over a bald corner of the garden, resulting in an exciting colourful display that 'they grew'.

of big bulbs, like hyacinths or daffodils, can be left sticking out the top; smaller ones should be completely covered.

Now, put the bowls or pots in a cool, moist and dark spot — a cupboard, a cellar, or moist shaded part of the garden — and leave it for six to eight weeks. If you are unable to find a suitable spot, then copy specialist nurseries and good gardeners and wrap the containers in black plastic and sink them in a moist, shaded part of the garden. Mark the spot with a stake so you do not forget where it is! Check the bowl regularly to make sure the compost is still damp. This method of wrapping it in plastic helps retain moisture and saves constant watering.

Root growth will be indicated when the tips of the leaves are showing about 3 to 6 centimetres. Under normal conditions, this will take about eight weeks but the pre-planting refrigeration will accelerate the process. When the leaf shoots are well developed, say, about 10 centimetres long, you can bring the bowl into a lighted room — preferably on a coolish, sunny window sill. If the room is too warm, the stems will grow too quickly and require staking. Keep moist but not soggy at all times. To make your bowl of bulbs really beautiful, sprinkle alyssum or bent grass seed over the surface once you have brought it into the warmth and light.

When the bulbs have finished blooming, pick off the dead flowers but let the stems and leaves die back naturally. This way they feed the bulb for the following year. (Tulips are usually discarded.) Tip the bulbs from the container and plant outside. They will not flower well next year, needing a season to recuperate, but will come up nicely the year after that. New bulbs will have to be bought for next year's project.

Potpourri

This well-known term refers to scented dried leaves and flowers, combined with a fixative, which are enjoyed for their long-lasting fragrance. There are two popular methods: dry potpourri and moist potpourri. Keep an eye out for antique lidded sugar bowls,

Potpourri can be displayed in decorative dishes and bowls throughout the house

pretty serving dishes, silver trays or unusual jars in which to display your potpourri.

Eleanour Sinclar Rohde wrote in *The Scented Garden* that, '. . . no bought potpourri is so pleasant as that made from one's own garden, for the petals of the flowers hold the sunshine and memories of summer, and . . . only the sunny days should be remembered.'

Harvest your potpourri flowers and leaves mid-morning, after the dew has dried, but before the sun has become too hot overhead. Place them on racks lined with paper and dry them in a slow oven. Using your hands, combine ingredients in a large glazed terracotta or earthenware pot. Then mix in orris root powder and essential oils, to personal preference, one drop at a time. You might like to add a few drops of brandy to strengthen the scent. Place the mixture in a dark, airtight container and store for a month to mature, gently shaking the contents regularly.

Tip

Children love the funny sensitive plant, *Mimosa pudica*. Teach them how to run their fingertips gently over the leaves, causing them to quickly close together in pairs.

You might like to use your potpourri to fill pretty sachets. Hang them wherever they may be brushed against or where passersby will occasionally squeeze them to release the scent. Use a variety of fabrics to make your sachets — gingham, sprigged cottons and embroidered lawn are all suitable — and experiment with shapes and sizes, too. Try the following recipe:

ROSE POTPOURRI

A warm, sweet mood-setter.

- 125 g red rose petals
- 75 g jasmine flowers
- 30 g orange flowers
- 12 bay leaves, crushed
- 4 tablespoons lavender
- 30 g sandalwood chips (from health food stores or chemists)
- 4 tablespoons cardamom seeds, crushed
- 2 teaspoons cinnamon
- 1 tablespoon crushed cloves
- 1 tablespoon crushed orange peel
- 3–4 tablespoons orris root powder
- essential oils of rose or musk

Scented Pillows

The Romans were the first to add dried rose petals to pillows, while Elizabethan mattresses were usually padded with Our Lady's Bedstraw (*Galium verum*). George III was said to rely upon a hop-scented pillow to '. . . relieve him from that protracted wakefulness under which he laboured for so long a time.'

Victorian ladies delighted in lavender cushions, turning their faces towards the sweet scent to avert a fainting attack.

Fragrant, flower-filled pillows delicately perfume the bedroom, calm jangled nerves and soothe fractious babies. Pretty, scented sachets also have a place in the home. Hang them

Scented pillows are a lovely addition to a bedroom; they also make pretty gifts

wherever they may occasionally be brushed against or where passersby will be tempted to squeeze them to release their scent. Gingham, sprigged muslin, organza and fine lawn are all suitable, and may be decorated with old-fashioned cross-stitch designs or embroidered initials. The filmy fabrics tend to look very feminine and possibly suit the sweeter-scented mixtures. Earthier colours like tan and bronze look smart filled with spice mixtures, as do stripes and paisleys; the latter make for very attractive masculine gifts. Simplest of all — and easy for children to make — is the lace handkerchief pillow, made by sewing two lace-trimmed handkerchiefs together with the frill outermost; use this as the decorative pillow cover. Experiment with different shapes and sizes.

Do not put herb and flower mixtures directly into the decorative cushion cover. Instead, make a case of closely woven material that is sewn up on three sides with a gap on the fourth side to enable you to turn it inside out. After doing this, put the mixture into the case and sew up the open seam before placing it in the decorative pillow case.

If the pillow is likely to be used as a sleeping pillow and not just as a decorative item, it is best made from soft fabric and not overfilled with wadding or potpourri mix. Fillings for scented sleeping pillows can be quite specific to their owner: eucalyptus leaves or rosemary for a person who suffers from asthma or other respiratory problems; thyme or lavender for someone who gets headaches regularly, and marjoram, lemon verbena or hops for those who have difficulty getting to sleep in the first place.

Chamomile is said to ward off nightmares and peppermint is good for travel sickness.

In the recipe provided here, crush flowers and herbs together in a bowl, mixing thoroughly but gently, then mix in two to three drops of the essential oil of your choice, and the required amount of orris root powder (from your chemist). You might also like to add a few drops of brandy to strengthen the scent. Many of the herbs and flowers may be harvested from your own garden or that of a neighbour and dried for future use. Some plants, like scented geraniums, need to be pruned regularly, so get into the habit of hanging the cut branches under cover (in the laundry, cellar or garage, for example) then you can crumble the leaves when they are dry and either store them in a bag or use them to make the scented pillow mixture straightaway, or even just to refresh any existing bowls of potpourri around the house. Lavender, rosemary, roses and lemon verbena are all easy to store in the same way.

SPICE PILLOW

A tangy, refreshing and slightly sharp mixture.

- 30 g lavender
- 30 g rose petals
- 15 g rose pelargonium leaves
- 15 g spearmint leaves
- 1 teaspoon cloves
- 2 teaspoon allspice berries, crushed
- 15 g teaspoon nutmeg, grated
- 1 tablespoon crushed cinnamon
- 1 tablespoon orris root powder
- essential oil of lavender

Other ingredients, such as the spices, can be readily bought from a delicatessen or supermarket. Your local health food store will often stock dried herbs, such as chamomile, which are sold ground or whole for tea.

Everlasting Flower Arrangements

Of all the crafts associated with the family garden, one of the most delightful is the preservation and display of flowers and foliage. Blossom picked in high summer and leaves gathered in autumn can be pressed and used to make lovely collage pictures. Larger flowers and sprays of leaves can be preserved by drying. If dried correctly, bunches of flowers retain their colour well and make really cheerful decorations in the winter months. Fresh flowers and leaves such as goldenrod, strawflowers, red and blue sage, cockscomb, golden celosia and pearly everlasting may all be dried for rich winter bouquets. After they are dry and their colours have set they will not fade, even if the arrangement is placed in a sunny spot. Flowers like angelica, teasel and artichoke are grown especially for drying and use in interior decoration. Most are usually hardy or half-hardy annuals and known as 'everlasting' plants, or by the lovely French name, *Immortelles*. You make like to grow some flowers specifically for drying in your family garden, too. Suggestions would include *Helipterum roseum*, the well-known straw daisy, *Ammobium alatum* the everlasting sand flower, globe amaranth or bachelor's buttons, and statice, or sea lavender, all of which grow up to 60 centimetres.

If you love having fresh flowers in the home, stretch your flower budget with dried foliage. Plumes of pampas grass, for instance, can be used to supplement an arrangement featuring just a few fresh flowers. Of course, do not put the dried flowers in the water. Dried hydrangea blooms or a dried mullein head or sweetpea vine can all be used in conjunction with fresh foliage to create eyecatching arrangements. You can also dry grasses for decoration, make pressed flower pictures and greeting cards, make leaf skeletons or use dried seeds and grasses to make hanging decorations, swags or wreaths.

There are several methods of drying and the simplest require no equipment. Some flowers dry naturally if left standing in water in a warm room until the water has evaporated, for example, delphiniums, goldenrod and hydrangea. Another simple method is air-drying, which works well for larkspur and Chinese lanterns and for seed heads like gladioli, poppy heads, iris pods, oats and quaking grass. Dry flowers in a dark, airy spot. Hang straight-stemmed materials in bundles, heads down, from lines. You can cut the stems later to the length you need. For curved stems, dry tall grasses in kegs, jugs or bottles; these will make for far more interesting arrangements.

Hang cut flowers upside down in an airy room to dry

Always gather flowers and grasses when they are dry but not too mature so the colour stays strong. Hang the flowers in small bunches in a dry, airy place protected from direct sunlight — a garage or carport could be a good position. A worthwhile tip to remember to prevent seed heads, berries or pods from dropping as they dry is to spray them with hair lacquer. This works especially well with holly berries and rosehips.

Borax may be used to preserve flowers and it has the added advantage of heightening their colour, though it also tends to make them a bit fragile. It is a good method to use for preserving marigolds or roses. Place the flowers in a shallow cardboard box on a layer of powdered borax; cover completely with more borax. Replace the lid and leave in a warm, dry place, such as an airing cupboard. Do not remove the flowers until they are papery to the touch — this can take up to ten days at least.

Another successful way to preserve foliage and seed heads is to stand them in a jar or wide-mouthed jug filled with a 1:2 mixture of glycerine and hot water. Evergreen leaves like ivy produce rich, glossy colours when preserved this way. Deciduous leaves, such as maple and oak, can also be treated this way. Pick them while they are green, not when they are changing colour. Remove any discoloured leaves and slit the base of the stem lengthways about 1 centimetre from the bottom. Stand the stems in the glycerine mixture. Inspect the leaves frequently to make sure they do not become saturated. When liquid begins to ooze out of the surface of the leaves, remove them, wipe them thoroughly and store in a dry, airy place.

Now that you have a selection of dried grasses, leaves, seed heads and flowers, you can make colourful arrangements in a variety of containers. If you are putting the flowers in a lightweight container, it is a good idea to put dry sand or gravel in the bottom of the container to give weight and stability to the arrangement. Knead a suitable amount of plasticine, dry 'oasis' foam (available from florists), or any other special material — such as plastic-coated wire mesh — available from craft shops. Place the material in the base of the container and crisscross it with strong rubber bands or fine wire. Push the ends of the dried plants into the base material to give the desired arrangement.

Things to Do

Children love experimenting with plants. One project I recall as a child was learning about the effect of sunlight on plants. For this activity, take a small pot plant, such as a geranium, and cover one leaf with tissue paper, taping it into place gently so as not to bruise the leaf. After a week, take the tissue away and you will see how the leaf has lost its green colour as a result of being deprived of sunlight.

Herb and Spice Wreaths

Wreaths are very beautiful, as well as practical, in home decoration. In ancient days wreaths also carried great symbolic significance, the perfect circle supposedly being a device to bring good fortune and ward off evil. Wreaths are relatively easy to make, a few inexpensive items may be purchased from a craft shop or department store and herbs and flowers may be picked in the family garden.

The canes pruned from grape vines can be woven together easily to form the basis for a wreath and they look so attractive they may not need decoration. If you do not have grape vines, try wisteria, willow or birch stems, or you can buy a wreath base. These are usually made from grape vines, raffia, straw, cane or thick wire and are usually circular or heart-shaped. Readymade wreath-bases are convenient, relatively inexpensive and may be used immediately. Other alternatives include sturdy wire, oasis rings and ones made from crumpled wire mesh. As the finished wreath is usually at least 5 centimetres larger than the base all round, the size should be chosen accordingly.

The exposed canes and stems give quite an interesting and pretty effect. Alternatively, you could prepare the wreath base by filling the spaces with tightly packed, pliable sphagnum moss and scrap material to prevent light showing through, binding securely in place with fine string or raffia. If desired, disguise any such bindings and untidy end pieces by carefully tucking extra moss around them.

Decorate your wreath by tucking in tiny bunches of herbs, flowers and grasses. While the choice of plants is almost unlimited, the following are particularly appropriate for making wreaths. For foliage, use the mints, lemon balm, both green and purple basils, sages, tarragon,

Safety Tip

Fit childproof fences around your swimming pool or any ponds you may have in your garden.

lamb's ears, lavender and pine needles. Rosemary and sage turn a most attractive silvery grey and banksias dry to a soft pale fawn and work well as a background. For flowers and seeds, use roses, rosehips, poppies, marjoram, hyssop, sweet cicely, lady's mantle and gypsophila. When preparing the base of your wreath, start at one side and work around in layers, one bunch over another — this way all the herbs will travel in the same direction — overlapping to conceal the stems.

Add extra colour to the wreath with flowering herbs such as lavender or clove pinks, or bright plants like everlasting daisies or marigolds. The delicate oval seeds of sweet honesty and the lacy-edged crisp pods of love-in-the-mist provide a dainty contrast. Miniature cumquats and pomegranates provide interest; small oranges studded with cloves give off a sweet and spicy aroma, while daintily grouped bunches of cinnamon bark or vanilla pods create pretty contrasts.

For the really craft-oriented child, why not experiment with using leftover spices and leaves to create imaginative 'flowers', with 'petals' of bay leaves surrounding a central bud of a walnut or star anise, for instance, all held together securely with fast-setting clear craft glue.

For a seasonal theme, such as Christmas, nutmeg, mace, star anise and ginger lightly covered with a dusting of gold spray paint, add variety of texture and colour. A festive wreath like this can be made even more colourful by intertwining plaid ribbons in between the canes and around and over the base itself.

To finish your herb or flower wreath, glue or tie a loop of satin ribbon in a complementary colour to the top of the wreath, by which it can be hung. If the wreath is particularly heavy, a sturdy wire loop should be attached to the back of the wreath at the top, where it cannot be seen.

Try misting the wreath with an essential oil, such as rose or carnation, diluted in pure alcohol, giving it a fresh, long-lasting fragrance.

A herb and spice wreath makes a beautiful, scented decoration, especially at Christmas time

A Wildflower Candle

Purchased candles are a little impersonal as a gift, but home-made ones, decorated with flowers and herbs, are a pleasure to make and receive. I particularly like the type that have dried flowers just showing through the translucent outer layer of wax. They can reflect the season, convey a personal message with their scent or colour, or simply match the recipient's favourite room. Making candles today is much simpler and safer than it once was — wax, wicks, colourings and a wide variety of decorative moulds are all readily available from craft suppliers.

---

350 g wax*

35 g stearin

few drops of perfume or flower essence, if desired, e.g. honeysuckle essence, peppermint, thyme or rose oil or rosewater, pinch of powdered sandalwood or clove powder

colouring powder or liquid to colour candles, if desired, e.g. turmeric, cochineal

30 g dried pressed flowers or herbs, e.g. pansies, violas, ferns, honeysuckle, rose petals, thyme, snipped rosemary, mint leaves, germander, hyssop or bergamot (bee balm)

vegetable oil

---

*Odourless paraffin wax is easily obtainable from craft stores. It is cheap, burns safely and well, and can be coloured and perfumed nicely. Read the accompanying instructions carefully. Most, but not all, brands will recommend combining the wax with stearin as described here. Stearin will help distribute the colour more evenly throughout the finished candle.

Alternatively, you can purchase plain candles (it is too difficult to make flowers stick to fluted ones) and decorate them with a garland or design of trailing flowers and leaves. Either attach flowers with a water-based glue and brush over them with a little clear melted wax, or briefly dip the candles into hot water to soften the wax and press a design of flowers and leaves directly into the softened surface.

Prepare the candle moulds according to the manufacturer's instructions. There will be six to 12 moulds in a set, depending on the size and shape of candle you want. Insert wicks, tying them at one end to a matchstick so that the wick hangs directly down the centre of the mould and the matchstick is flush across the open mould end. This means you will not lose the wick once the wax is poured in — you can easily trim it to a more manageable length later. If wicks are not included in a kit, ask for advice on the best kind to buy; a wick that is too thick will smoke unpleasantly.

Melt the wax in the top half of a non-aluminium double boiler over simmering water. Melt the stearin in a second double boiler and add it to the wax. Stir in perfume or flower essence and add enough powder or colouring liquid to give the candles a rich colour. With purchased dye, combine according to manufacturer's instructions, either as a ready-prepared powder or grated from a tablet of craft dye. Alternatively, you can experiment with the dyes already available in your kitchen. Ground turmeric, for instance, gives a lovely bright golden yellow. A good tip to remember is to select a colour that will echo the choice of perfume and floral decoration for your candle. A clear glowing yellow suggests lemon thyme; a pink candle could be perfumed with rose essence and feature rose petals, while soft pink and green could be used for a jasmine-scented candle.

Mould the candles and allow them to set. Keep a little of the wax aside. When the candles are firm, re-melt half of the reserved wax, paint

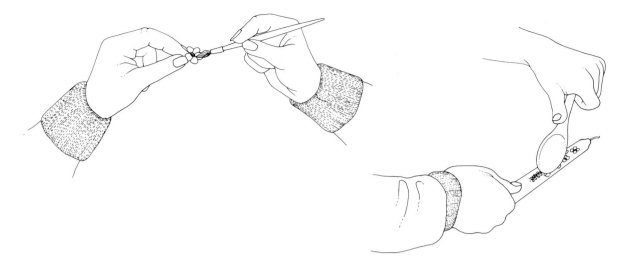

1. Paint the backs of the flowers and leaves with a little melted wax and press them onto the candle in the desired pattern.

2. Gently 'iron' over the flowers and leaves to secure them in place, then carefully paint over the flowers and leaves with a little melted wax.

the backs of the wildflowers, petals or dried ferns and press firmly into a pattern around each candle. 'Iron' the leaves or flowers into place by smoothing the candle wax gently with a warmed dry spoon. (If the spoon is too hot it will scorch the flower decoration or pull it off the candle; if it is too cool it will not really help, while an even slightly damp one will lift off the flowers and ruin it.) If you are using quite large or heavy pieces, or trying to secure a thick stem, for instance, hold it in place with small pins or tiny pieces of florist's wire. It is possible to nip off the ends of fine-grade dressmaking pins with a pair of pliers and push them right in so the ends do not show.

Paint over the top of the flowers with the reserved wax, or heat a long mould or tin half-filled with clear paraffin wax and dip the candles once or twice until a thin transparent glaze appears on the flowers. Place the whole item in a cold water bath to cool it more quickly, if necessary; leave to harden. If the candle is difficult to remove from its mould, place it in the refrigerator for at least 30 minutes. Some moulds are metal; other newer ones are made from plastic and 'unlock' to release the candle, reducing the risk of cracking or breakage.

Using low-temperature beeswax instead of — or in conjunction with — paraffin wax gives candles a rich tawny yellow colour. Beeswax also enhances the scent of the burning candle with its natural honeyed scent. However, it is usually more expensive than paraffin wax.

Things to Do

Make rosemary bookmarks by mounting sprigs of dried rosemary on stiff parchment or coarse linen. Dried cornflowers and delphiniums both keep their colour well and look attractive with the grey-green rosemary. Cover the bookmark with clear self-adhesive plastic, finishing the edges with bias binding, lace or grosgrain. ribbon. Glue or tie a length of matching ribbon or silk cord on the top. As a bonus for the book lover, rosemary's strong scent helps keep moths and silverfish at bay.

Pressed Flower Pictures

Children love learning how to make pressed flower pictures. The following flowers, leaves and grasses are particularly suitable for pressing:

Flowers: buttercup, clematis, daisy, delphinium, larkspur, goldenrod, hydrangea florets, pansy, roses, fuchsia and wattle. Yellow and orange flowers press well and retain their colour, especially marbretia, wattle, marigolds and daffodils. (*Note:* with daffodils and many other trumpet-shaped or bell-shaped flowers, remove the thick seed box under the head and slit the flowers down the centre with a razor blade. This gives a more manageable 'flower' of three petals and half a trumpet for pressing.)

Leaves: ferns, geranium, gingko, liquidambar, maybush, blackberry, grevillea, ivy, clematis, yarrow, maple, eucalyptus, parsley, chamomile leaf, lavender or Virginia creeper. Ivy leaves will turn brown with pressing as do most ferns. *Centaurea* and *cineraria* have grey leaves which are quite beautiful and do not change colour

Preserve the flowers from your garden by making your own pressed flower pictures

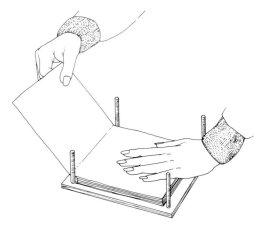

1. *Place four layers of blotting or other absorbent paper in a flower press, folding the top layer in half as shown.*

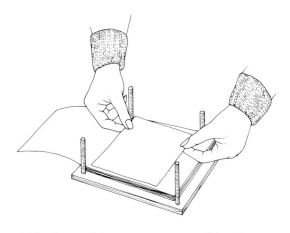

2. *Add a layer of tissue paper on top of these layers.*

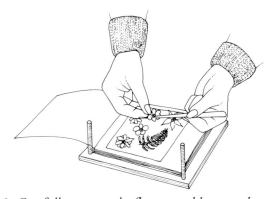

3. *Carefully arrange the flowers and leaves to be pressed on top of the tissue paper, ensuring that they do not overlap.*

4. *Cover the flowers and leaves with a layer of tissue paper then fold the blotting paper over. Cover with another four layers of blotting paper and secure the press.*

with pressing. Beech leaves can be picked when red or gold and will retain that colour when pressed.

Grasses: vanilla grass, quaking grass or barley. For pressing, always gather flowers, grasses, seed heads and leaves when they are dry, otherwise mould will form. Press material as soon as possible after gathering. Inexpensive flower presses are available at craft shops or you can use the traditional method of pressing flowers and plants between sheets of blotting paper, with either heavy books or ordinary bricks to weigh them down.

Prepare leaves, flowers and seeds separately for pressing and always discard any stems that are too thick. Instead, use those of primrose, clover or clematis as the 'stem' in the picture. To get the best results it is sometimes necessary to dismantle the flowers, for example, with roses, and press each petal separately. Then, after the petals have been pressed, they may be reassembled as a flower. When the coloured petals are delicate, for example, with a poppy, always lay two petals on top of each other. This will give them a deeper colour. If a flower has a very thick centre, like a marigold, press the centre firmly with your thumb to open out the petals evenly before laying it on the blotting paper.

Most leaves and flowers take at least one month to dry out properly, so do not be tempted to remove the weights too soon. If the thick-centred flowers appear not to be ready on first inspection, replace the blotting paper and press again for another two to three weeks. Your dried materials are ready for arranging when the petals feel right and no moisture is left in the paper layers. If they are not thoroughly dry when you take them from the press, the leaves will curl. You can store dried flowers and grasses by covering them with paper sacks or upturned boxes to keep them dust-free until you are ready to use them, either in a dried flower bouquet or pressed flower picture.

Once the flowers and grasses are ready, children can start to make their picture. For beginners, the best background material is black, white or coloured cardboard. They will also need a small paint-brush, scissors, practice paper, clear craft adhesive and an inexpensive framing kit, containing a frame, glass, backing board and backing sealer (for example, tape or paper and tacks).

Firstly, cut out a piece of practice paper the same size as the background material will be, so that the pressed flowers, leaves or grasses may be laid out in the desired design before being glued into place. Avoid too much handling of the flowers; use tweezers with a pointed end, if necessary, or use the paintbrush to shift them around the paper. Do not try to put too many

Lavender is easy to dry and retains its scent well. Once dry, it can be used in many different ways

pressed flowers in one pattern and try to retain the natural curve of any stalks or grasses.

When you are happy with the arrangement, transfer it to the background material and, when that arrangement is satisfactory, gently dab a little adhesive on the centre back of each piece with the tip of the brush handle and gently press into position with fingers or tweezers. When the picture is complete, press the glass down on top of it, secure with a weight and leave to set. Then fix the backing and glass into the frame proper, according to the manufacturer's instructions. With dried flower pictures, it is a good idea to cover the back completely with brown paper to protect it against moths, dust and possible mould.

Tip

Dried flower arrangements can present a fire risk. Never place arrangements above an open fire or near lighted candles on a dining table.

The garden is home to many creatures — some easier to see than others

5

ALL CREATURES GREAT AND SMALL

In the Dog House

K eeping a dog is a lot easier if you have a special place for it to live and sleep where it knows it can find the things it needs. For instance, any dog outdoors for more than a leashed walk each day needs a water dish handy. And, if your dog is like most mutts, tipping that dish over is just the funniest trick in the world, so it is preferable to arrange the dog's kennel and belongings in a spot that is not likely to get damp and soggy as a result.

Before building or purchasing a dog kennel, remember that animals in the wild move around and choose their own 'bedrooms' with light and air in mind. Keep the kennel off the ground, both to lessen the chance of wood rot and to provide a warmer floor in winter. It is a good idea to have some means of ventilating the kennel, too. Whether you are building the kennel or buying it, make sure it has either a removable roof or a side panel to facilitate

cleaning. There is nothing more infuriating than poking your arm through a dog-sized hole and futilely trying to clean up. This roof or panel should be hinged to prevent it from flying up in the wind.

The kennel floor should be either timber or covered with a firm, low-nap material, such as felt or a piece of old blanket. Some readymade dog kennels have a removable piece of seagrass or coir matting (from coconut husk), rather like a doormat, which is both sturdy and comfortable. Do not use metal or linoleum on the floor. Some veterinary surgeries have metal-floored cages for sick animals because they are easily cleaned and sterilised. However, they are far too cold for regular use. Pay particular attention to roofing specifications. A watertight shelter will keep your pet safely out of the wind and cold when you are not at home.

When siting a dog kennel, try to do so from

Tip

Take children with you to the nursery to select 'their' plants. You may be surprised to see what they like and to hear why. Plants which children love to play with may include:

- Lamb's ears (*Stachys lanata*) — soft and velvety, just like a lamb's ear, in fact.
- Moses-in-a-basket (*Rhoeo spathacea*) — with its dear little 'baby' flower nestled in the leaves (mostly grown as a house plant).
- Angel's fishing rod (*Dierama pulcherrimum*) — for its intriguing name as much as for its very pretty bell-shaped pink flowers.
- Foxgloves for doll's hats, naturally. (Beware, though, this is a poisonous plant.)
- Shrimp bush (*Beloperone guttata*) — with its pink prawn-like flowers; ditto the goldfish plant (*Nematanthus wettsteinii*), a relative of the African violet, with its fat gold flowers 'swimming' in the leaves

summer breeze, but do not be surprised if, on a really hot day, it will dig itself a wallow in the cool earth of your favourite flowerbed. Kennels are probably most desirable in winter when the close-fitting space helps to conserve body heat. In warm weather, however, your dog needs to have enough room to be able to move around in the kennel. Some readymade models have an optional draft partition or baffle, providing the best of both worlds.

To make a dog kennel fit your dog, you first need to know exactly how big your dog is and, importantly, how big it will be when it is fully grown. The dog must be able to turn around and stand up in the kennel. Make a note of its length, height and width. Importantly, try to catch it asleep and measure how far its body and legs spread out on the floor. As a general rule, the length of the kennel should be one-and-a-third times the length of the dog, its width should be one-and-a-half times the shoulder height of the dog and its height should be one-and-a-third times the head height of the dog. When working out the size of the doorway, just add several centimetres to the height and width of your dog all around.

If you are building the dog kennel as a project, begin construction with the floor frame, creating a raised floor and then nailing a plywood sheet to the upper edges of the frame. The floor of the kennel must be at least 10 centimetres off the ground to allow the circulation of air. Mark outlines for two end panels on plywood to the necessary height and width.

To create a sloping roof, mark off a point in the centre of the plywood which is double the height required and connect this point with the tops of the sides which are the regular height. Carefully saw out shapes. Cut a doorway in the bottom centre of one of the end walls. Cut air vents (decoratively shaped, if you fancy) near the peaks of the end walls. Then attach the two end walls to the floor frame with nails.

Cut two side walls, bevelling one side of each at a 45-degree angle and attach the side walls with the angle facing inwards. Fasten two roof

the dog's point of view. If your dog lives mainly out of doors, do not confuse it by letting it sleep inside some of the time. On the other hand, if you live in a garden flat or townhouse, your dog really does not need a kennel. Just convert one end of the verandah or patio into accommodation for it by installing a wooden deck, perhaps with a screen against the wind.

Position the kennel or sleeping deck so that your pet can enjoy the cooling effects of any

panels made from sloping sheets by
nailing all the way around, through
the end roof panels and the upper
angled edges of the side walls.
When you do this, you should
allow for an overhang at the front
to keep out the rain. Now apply
any decorative roofing material and
finish you desire. Round off any
corners to minimise the risk of
injury to your pet.

Careful attention to small
details will make the dog kennel an
attractive feature in the family
garden. For instance, adhesive
shingles can be applied over the
roof for an appealing look. A neat
paint job, say red and yellow, can
make the dog kennel look cheerful,
but wait until the paint is dry
before letting the dog anywhere near it!
Use unleaded paint as some dogs enjoy chewing
on paintwork. A useful accessory is a metal
ring, firmly attached to the front wall near the
door. Tie your pup to this if you are training it
to use the kennel.

*1. Begin construction with
the floor, which should be
raised at least 10 cm off
the ground.*

*2. Attach the end panels
to the floor with nails. Cut
decorative patterns in the
top of these panels to act as
ventilation holes.*

*3. Attach two side walls, one
side of each bevelled inwards
at 45°, to the floor with
nails, bevelled side inward.*

*4. Securely attach the two
roof panels by nailing all the
way around and decorate as
desired.*

Butterfly Gardening

The family garden belongs not only to you, but also to the hundreds of insects, worms, caterpillars and birds to whom it is home, recreation area and foodsource. The family garden should be a refuge for insects and, while it may be difficult to convince a keen gardener that aphids and thrips play an important part in a garden's ecosystem, everybody loves butterflies!

With the right kind of flowers and the right sort of caterpillar food to begin with, butterflies can add a new dimension of pleasurable colour and movement to the family garden. Of the many hundreds of varieties, some of the more common butterflies you may see include the orchard butterfly (*Papilio aegeus*), dingy swallowtail (*Papilio anactus*), blue triangle (*Graphium starpedon*), the common jezebel (*Delias nigrina*) of eastern Australia, the Ulysses butterfly (*Papilio ulysses joesa*) of the northern rainforests and the common brown (*Heteronympha merope merope*), found in southeastern and Western Australia, along with the Australian admiral (*Vanessa itea*). The wanderer (*Danaus plexippus*) is originally from North America but is now one of 'our' most common and pretty species. The chequered swallowtail (*Papilio demoleus*) is widespread throughout mainland Australia, as are the painted lady (*Vanessa kershawi*) and the meadow argus (*Junonia viddida*). The common grass blue (*Zizina labradus*) is probably the most common butterfly to be found in Australian gardens, especially wherever clover grows. Not to be encouraged, however, is the introduced cabbage white butterfly (*Pierie rapae*) whose larvae will decimate any vegetable garden nearby, especially broccoli, cauliflower and, as its name suggests, cabbages.

Of course, butterflies start out as caterpillars, which can have voracious appetites, but if your family garden is to be a sanctuary for butterflies, you will have to be willing to tolerate the odd tattered leaf. Also, the garden must be insecticide-free. Some pioneering organic gardeners recommend a hidden 'wild spot' of caterpillar food plants be included at the garden planning stage, perhaps in a neglected corner which is not so noticeable. The favourite leaf foods of many caterpillars include blood flower (*Asclepias curvassavica*), and other milkweeds, rue, cassia, parsley and oleander (but this is not advisable if children are likely to make contact with its poisonous sap).

Children, in particular, find butterflies fascinating; they may even like to set up a butterfly breeding farm. For this project, you will need a shoe box, some fine netting (shadecloth is ideal), a small garden pot full of slightly damp soil or potting mix, and a supply of the correct food plant for the larvae, or caterpillars. If you are observant, you will notice that butterflies and moths tend to remain in the area that contains their food plant. However, remember that caterpillars do not necessarily feed on the same plants as their parent butterflies or moths. For instance, the caterpillars of red admirals and tortoiseshell butterflies eat stinging nettles, while the butterflies themselves patronise nectar-rich flowers.

Collect small branches of the plant or shrub where the larvae was first found and push them into the pot. Cut out one of the long sides of the shoe box and cut netting to cover; stitch or staple it into place. Place the pot and food plant into the box and gently put the larvae onto the leaves. (Remember that caterpillars have no bones and

Safety Tip

Never leave lengths of rope lying about the garage or garden where children can find them.

are easily squashed — try to roll the caterpillar out into the box and onto the leaves, rather than picking it up between thumb and finger.) Put the lid back on the shoe box, securing it with a light weight or rubber band if it is likely to be tipped up by other children, for instance. Replace the plant material with fresh branches every day and clean up any caterpillar droppings. The larvae should soon turn into a chrysalis and, after that, the butterfly or moth will emerge. Children should not touch the new insect until its wings are quite dry. When it is starting to flutter about the box, take the box back out to shrub or plant where the larvae was first found, take the lid off and let it leave when it is ready. If

it does not immediately fly away, *gently* ease your finger under its feet and pop it on a leaf so it can safely prepare itself for flight.

For those who want to see more butterflies fluttering in their gardens, plant flowers and shrubs with brightly coloured flowers, particularly pink and red, blue, yellow and mauve. It has been found that certain types of butterflies prefer one colour over another and some will seek out a preferred colour over very considerable distances. Even brightly painted pebbles and flower pots will interest a butterfly.

Fragrance is equally important to butterflies and many of the plants they favour have strong, sweet scents. Lavender is a classic plant for

The wanderer butterfly (Danaus plexippus*)*

Buddleia davidii, *commonly referred to as the 'butterfly bush'*

this energy. Some butterflies dine on a diet of pollen, which is rich in protein. These butterflies excrete an enzyme which breaks down the pollen to form a sort of 'pollen soup' which they then suck up with their straw-like proboscises. Nectar is the preferred food of most adult butterflies and, so they can quickly and easily insert their long 'tongue' into that nectar, they will seek out those plants that typically have flowers with long tubular calyces, each with a pool of nectar at the base of a groove or channel. These narrow tubes tend to keep less desirable insects from stealing the nectar. Butterflies prefer flowers that provide a perch, too, so they

drawing them to the garden, as are buddleia and the fleshy ice plant (*Sedum*) which has big flat heads of tiny pink flowers that act as a magnet for butterflies. All the sedums are attractive to butterflies; sedums love full sun and thrive on heat, making them the perfect choice for a sun-filled family garden. *Buddleia davidii,* in fact, is commonly known throughout the world as the 'butterfly bush' because when it is in full bloom it is seldom without several butterfly visitors perched on the showy, scented flower spikes. Buddleias flower from early summer to late autumn and will be visited by clouds of wanderers, blue triangles and swallowtails. As well as the common purple variety, there are beautiful white-flowered buddleias ('White Profusion' and 'White Bouquet') and a richly coloured red ('Royal Red' and 'Orange Ball') with unusual honey-scented orange flowers.

Butterflies need plenty of carbohydrate to fuel their busy muscles and sweet nectar provides

may feed without expending too much valuable energy while hovering to eat. For this reason, you will note that quite a few of the plants favoured by butterflies, notably thyme, catmint, hyssop, yarrow, honeysuckle, wallflowers, buddleia and lantana, have either single flowers with a flattish rim or lip or a head of many flowers densely packed together.

Other flowers butterflies love include honeysuckle, Chilean jasmine (*Mandevilla*), jonquils, jasmine, wallflowers and lilacs. The closely packed flowers of veronica, verbena and phlox will attract butterflies as will daisies — particularly the Michaelmas daisy — asters and dahlias. Bright gold and orange marigolds, old-fashioned single chrysanthemums, single petunias and everlasting daisies are also attractive to butterflies. Certain Australian wildflowers may be brought into the garden to provide nectar for butterflies: rush lilies (*Sowerbaea*), boronias, bottlebrushes and many of the small-

Butterflies are a beautiful addition to any garden. They will be encouraged into your garden by the correct choice of plants

flowered grevillea varieties are much appreciated. The extremely beautiful and brilliantly coloured Fiery Jewel (*Hypochrysops ignitus*) will patronise the native cherry (*Exocarpos* spp.) and several species of acacia. Balsam or busy lizzies (*Impatiens*) are another garden favourite — the red-flowered varieties, in particular, will attract butterflies. The flat flowers provide a perfect feeding platform for dainty butterfly feet and there is plenty of nectar in the centre of each flower for a nice long drink.

Even that imported pest, the lantana, has a saving grace in that it attracts native butterflies. Lazy gardeners will be happy to learn that they are most likely to produce the best 'crop' of butterflies in a slightly overgrown garden, or one that is a little wild. Such a garden will probably contain weeds like Scotch thistle, white clover and milkweed, all of which attract butterflies.

Of course, dainty as they may seem, butterflies do not always dine on nectar. Some find rotting fruit, especially plums and guavas, absolutely irresistible, while professional butterfly catchers have been known to use manure to attract butterflies. Even human perspiration, which is high in salt, can be an attractant. Sodium (or salt), interestingly enough, is thought to play a role in the butterfly's sexual stimulation and egg production.

A final point to remember in butterfly gardening: butterflies will not feed or breed in a cold or windswept garden; they prefer a sheltered, warm area. Creating suntraps in gardens, either by erecting walls or hedges, will make for warm peaceful places that will be frequented by humans and butterflies alike. As a bonus, wind breaks will trap not only the sun, but the scent of the 'butterfly flowers'.

Worm Farming

You can be certain that what is valuable and exciting to children is not what you had envisaged when you planned the family garden. A good example is worms. Children love to explore and map out the complex web of life in a garden and, having been taught the value of worms, are quite likely to want to know more about them. Why not give in gracefully to fate and go the whole hog by installing a worm farm? You may even be able to turn your children's hobby to profit by selling them to the local fishing club, organic gardeners or nurseries.

The earthworms that are most common in Australia are *Aporrectodea caliginosa*, *A. longa*, *A. rosea* and *Lumbricus rubellus*. Gardeners love earthworms because they are good for the soil. (The only exception can be if they infest a potted plant — when worms set up residence in pots, the potting mix declines at an alarming rate. Generally just topping up with potting mix and compost will ensure the plant continues to flourish.) Worms break up organic materials, old root mats, and thick layers of leaf litter and mix them back into the soil, thus improving the nutrient content and 'crumble-ability' of the soil and, ultimately, allowing for better penetration of plant roots, oxygen and water into the soil. In addition to processing soil and organic material through their systems — earthworms eat at least half their own weight in soil each day — their movements in the soil also help increase plant growth by allowing for root, air and water penetration. Soil with plenty of earthworms in it is able to hold more water without getting waterlogged or turning sour, unlike soil from which they are absent.

Safety Tip

Never leave your car parked in the driveway without the handbrake on and never work on or under your car when your children are playing nearby; wait until they are asleep.

Earthworms do not like being impaled by forks, chopped up with spades or gobbled up by birds. Naturally, in gardens, some cultivation is necessary, but for earthworms to flourish, plenty of compost and mulch are required to protect the soil surface and, importantly, keep the soil cool and so extend the earthworms' activities into the hotter months of the year. Like all living things, earthworms need food: leaves, lawn clippings, well-mulched weeds and vegetable scraps all make for happy and healthy earthworms, as do compost and animal manure. (*Note:* earthworms do not like being sprinkled with fertiliser or dry manure as it will burn them. Fewer worms will be damaged by sprinkling fertiliser on the surface of the soil and watering it in well before digging.) Keep the soil moist at all times. Be careful not to overwater, or the soil will become saturated and the earthworm burrows will be flooded. Go easy on chemical sprays if you want plenty of earthworms. Research has shown that nematicides, ant and termite killers and fumigants are particularly lethal.

If you have decided to set up an earthworm farm, you will need a container (the foam cartons or wooden boxes used to pack fresh fruit and vegetables are ideal), bedding materials, food and, of course, earthworms. Bedding material can include peatmoss, shredded paper, leaf mould and a straw or grass clippings mixture, or a combination of all three. The bedding must be moistened until it is just possible to squeeze a few drops of water from it. To this layer, add a thin layer (5 centimetres) of soil, then another slightly thicker (10 centimetres) layer of compost, then sprinkle a bit more soil on top.

A good position for the box is the garage or garden shed or, in warm weather, outdoors in a sheltered area where it is protected from direct sun and, preferably, rain. Direct sun can make the box too hot for the worms, while the rain can make it too wet, possibly fouling the soil and killing the worms. If the box has to go outside, drainage holes must be provided.

Introduce worms to the box once the compost has cooled. You can start with just one or two pairs — it will not take long before there are a lot more! Before popping them into the box, bury some food for them. Almost any dead organic matter can be used: kitchen scraps, poultry pellets, seaweed, manure and leaves are all suitable. Large pieces, such as cabbage leaves and chunks of cauliflower, should be chopped up first. Put the worms on top of the soil over the buried food and they will soon wriggle downwards to escape the light. Cover the box loosely with shadecloth, hessian, or weed control matting to exclude light and reduce moisture loss. The amount you feed your earthworms can

be worked out by trial and error. Simply, the more worms there are, the greater their ability to dispose of uneaten kitchen scraps or manure. If you find that scraps are staying uneaten on the surface, then reduce the amount until the number of worms increases.

Other worm-farming management tips to remember are to check the aeration of the soil regularly by gently poking the surface with a fork every couple of weeks; sprinkling the soil with water every two to seven days, depending on the time of year, to maintain the correct moisture content and temperature (it must be cool, not hot), based on the 'squeeze test'. If your kids want to have nice fat worms to sell, they should feed them with poultry pellets or cornmeal. Also, test the pH of the soil every so often. It should be about six to eight and, if you are feeding the worms mainly with kitchen scraps, this may not be the case. Adding a few eggshells or a very light sprinkling of wood ashes or dolomite will correct the balance and stop the soil from souring.

Fish Ponds

How about a small fish pond in the family garden? This really is a fascinating addition for all the family to enjoy — children love to watch fish and tadpoles and adults might care to learn to cultivate exotic and often wonderfully scented water plants. Keeping fish is fun and the pond will reflect many nearby plants and rocks, making for an attractive feature. However, it must always be adequately protected by wire netting to prevent a young child's drowning. There are many different approaches and styles that could complement the rest of the garden. For instance, your fish pond could be a large cement-lined one with caves, cliffs and secret 'pirate harbours', made by heaping stones in the pool. Or, a pond could be included as part of a rockery or rock garden (see page 77). Make the rock garden from the soil dug out while excavating the pond.

Most gardening centres and specialist suppliers sell prefabricated ponds (see pages 69–70), usually made from concrete, fibrous concrete or fibreglass. They are available in a wide variety of shapes and sizes. The important point to remember when planning your fish pond, as opposed to a simple water feature, is that fish require *deep* water. Put your hand in a bucket of water standing in the backyard on a hot summer's day and see how warm it gets! Also, if you want movement in your fish pond by way of a fountain or waterfall, you will need a pump and a filter — make sure the filter is also netted, so as not to chew up any of your fish!

Make sure that the deeper part of the pond is watertight as the plants and fish that will occupy that section will not survive a loss of water. I consider the best style of fish pond, whether it is a purchased one or whether you are

constructing it yourself, should not be a uniform depth but rather have a curved or rectangular deeper section. This allows scope for water lilies in the deep water and smaller aquatic plants around the shallow edge. It creates a healthier environment for the fish, too.

Plant the pond with water weeds that grow quickly before stocking it with fish. Plant dwarf trees or shrubs around the edge. These should be in harmony with the pond shape and, therefore, look as though they have some affinity with water. Suggestions include the elephant's ear (*Colocasia antiquorum illustris*) which has very large shield-shaped leaves, the evergreen butterfly iris (*Moraea bicolor*) or the rather graceful striped leaves of *Miscanthus japonicus*. Flag irises are ideal edging plants for a fish pond as they will grow in and out of the water and will flower most of the summer.

Other plants which will do very well either in wet conditions or shallow water at the pond's edge include the iris-like *Acorus calamus* or sweet flag and the cape pond flower (*Aponogeton*

distachyos), which are both sweetly fragrant. Several of the mints will happily grow up to and into the water; *Mentha requienii*, or Corsican mint, makes a bouncy bright green mat that will drape itself mossily around damp rocks and into shady crevices, creating a cool peppermint-scented haven to which a child may retreat to daydream. I also like the graceful *Cyperus papyrus*, or papyrus, of Ancient Egyptian fame, with its feathery scented leaves and the pretty little floating heart (*Limnanthemum peltatam*), which grows like a water lily with floating leaves and flowers. The floating heart only needs about 15 to 45 centimetres of water, making it suitable for even a very tiny pond. Water lilies, even though they are the first plants to come to mind when planning a fish pond, are usually extremely vigorous; even the pygmy varieties will require at least 1.2 square metres of water surface.

Most nurseries will stock rushes (*Juncus* spp.) but I do not recommend these for fish ponds as they tend to be very vigorous and could easily overwhelm other plants in the pond. Many of

You may be fortunate enough to be able to incorporate a large pond into your garden

the bulrushes (*Scirpus* spp.) are also highly invasive and will spread very enthusiastically. Their roots can be checked to some extent by planting them in containers but they are really only suitable for the margins of very large ponds. Better choices include water milfoil (*Myriophyllum proserpinacoides*), with its extremely decorative trailing feathery leaves with tips that turn red in autumn and the lovely blue-flowered *Pontederia cordata* or pickerel weed.

It is important to include some submerged aquatic plants in a fish pond for two reasons. Firstly, they help to oxygenate the water and maintain its clarity and freshness; secondly, they provide safe areas where the fish can lay their eggs and, later, where the young fry can hide from their parents' cannibalistic tendencies. Their growth must be controlled, as with all water plants, or else they will grow rampantly and compete for the light and warmth of the sun, forming masses that trap the fish near the surface where birds can quickly pick them off. Pondweed is probably the most widely available type of submerged aquatic plant. Look for *Potamogeton crispus*, which has narrow leaves, but steer clear of the floating *P. natans*, which can completely cover and choke out a pond.

When arranging plants in the fish pond do not introduce any of the organic material you would normally use with land plants. Leaf mould, compost and peat will give off too many mineral salts as they break down and these can encourage algae which, in turn, can discolour the water and suffocate the fish. Ponds without soil need to have oxygenating plants introduced in containers. Fill shallow boxes or pots with soil and cow manure or special fertiliser and a little charcoal to help stop the water from souring. Having stocked your pond with plants, introduce the fish and water snails to complete the balanced community.

To avoid disappointment, always check with the supplier when you buy your fish and ask about any special requirements they may have so you can ensure the pond is chemically and thermally suitable. It is possible to buy water-testing kits and the chemicals necessary to adjust the quality of the water. In concrete-lined pools, for instance, certain chemicals will be leached into the water over time, but this is easily corrected. However, before deciding on concrete, consider a pre-fabricated or PVC pool, which generally present fewer of these problems.

The problem of a fish pond freezing over is less likely to occur in most parts of Australia or New Zealand but, if you live in a colder climate, a heating system will be required. The simplest way to heat a fish pond is with thermostatically controlled electric immersion heaters, but these are really only for the serious enthusiast as they are quite expensive. A cheaper alternative would be a black absorption plate 'thermal collector' which can be connected to a pump, warming the water as it passes through.

Children will usually enjoy learning about all the additional wildlife that will be attracted to their fish pond: dragonflies, frogs and water beetles, just to name a few. It is pleasant to sit outside on a warm spring evening and be able to hear 'your' frog calling for a mate and then later to see frog spawn and tiny tadpoles darting about. Mosquitoes, unfortunately, will also enjoy visiting your fish pond, though the fish make short work of the majority of mosquito larvae. Aphids, which enjoy snacking on soft water plants, will also be kept in check by the fish. Help matters along by dislodging the aphids from the plants with a powerful jet of water or a syringe. Never use chemical sprays near the water, as they will almost inevitably kill the fish. Birds and bees will also use the fish pond for eating so make sure the fish have plenty of leaves and plants to hide beneath. Building a little overhanging rock ledge around the pool's perimeter will provide shelter and a cool retreat on a hot day.

Safety Tip

Ensure your clothes line is set at a higher level than your child can reach.

Native Animals in the Garden

The best way to attract and retain wildlife in any area is to provide the type of environment which they like. Some animals like dense vegetation, some like open spaces, while others like low, bushy shrubs. The type of plants used and the way they are set out will vary greatly according to what animals or birds you are planning to encourage and the part of the world in which you live. Always consult someone who is knowledgeable about the plants and wildlife in your area.

It is desirable, when planning a family-oriented garden, to create at least some places where animals can retreat from man and from predators, such as domestic cats and dogs — and children — such as tall trees or very bushy areas or even, if space permits, a meshed-off 'wild corner'. You can institute a regular feeding program to entice the animals from their refuge. Be careful, though, not to overfeed them to the point where any animals or birds become too dependent on you.

Australia's towns and cities are home to an abundance of native wildlife. Many species of animals, including possums and fruit bats, skinks and even echidnas, along with blue tongue lizards, cicadas and tree frogs, all form an important part of urban ecology. Given the current worldwide concern about the conservation of wildlife, it is worthwhile encouraging your family's interest in the native animals that live in your neighbourhood. By better understanding their needs, you can protect and enhance the natural areas that remain, both for the benefit of the animals and for your own enjoyment.

In an area surrounded by bush, the echidna will sometimes find its way into the garden

Let's look at some of the more common urban wildlife species that you might be lucky enough to attract to your family's garden. (*Note:* native birds are discussed on page 165)

The Australian echidna is one of only two mammals in the world that lays eggs, the other being the platypus. While platypuses are extremely good at not being seen, preferring to stay in remote waterways, it is quite possible if you live near bushland that you might see an echidna waddling across the front lawn. Echidnas have a special fondness for insects such as ants and termite larvae and will often be under logs or shrubs where this food is to be found. When the weather gets colder and ants and termites are scarce, the echidna will hibernate for a month or so. This is when you are most likely to find one that may have burrowed down into a flowerbed for some peace and quiet. They are better off in the bush, especially if you or a neighbour have a dog that might pester them. To remove the echidna, *gently* slide a flat-blade spade underneath it, scooping down into the surrounding earth so as not to harm its soft little feet and nose. Be sure to wear gloves — those spines are sharp — and watch out for the long claw on the back of its foot.

Other marsupials you may come across if you live in a country area are dunnarts, mouse-like creatures which live on a diet of insects and spiders; antechinus, which are carnivorous marsupials like quolls; bandicoots, which are nocturnal creatures, retreating to the shelter of any nearby bushland during the day. Gardeners will quickly know whether there is a bandicoot nearby because they dig conical-shaped holes in lawns in an attempt to get at earthworms and burrowing larvae. Bandicoots are becoming

scarcer these days, due to increasing pressure from domestic cats and dogs. If you are concerned about a bandicoot's welfare in your neighbourhood, ask a representative from the National Parks and Wildlife Service to come and transport it to a safe haven nearby. Like possums, bandicoots make their presence felt with the unearthly squeals they make, usually late at night.

Surveys by National Parks and Wildlife rangers indicate that possums are usually far more common than expected in any area. Being small, nocturnal and fairly nimble, they have coped with urban development quite well. In fact, Telecom engineers often report on possums that have set up house in junction boxes! Sadly, you may also occasionally see an electrocuted possum hanging from powerlines. Some ringtail possums have been known to live in chimneys or attics but, by and large, they prefer to make their dome-shaped nests in the forks of trees or in thick brush. There are three main families of possums: the ringtails, the brushtails and the pygmy possums. Of these, you are most likely to see members of the first two groups, particularly if your house is near bushland or a large, treed park.

Ringtail possums have small, appealing faces with short round ears and a long tapering tail with a white tip. Brushtails have greyish or reddish fur and are solidly built with large ears and a dark bushy tail. We tend to see quite a few possums around our area because the local council has planted a great many flowering banksias and possums favour the pollen-rich blossoms. Possums also eat leaves and fruit and, as rose enthusiasts will grimly attest, they have a taste for new flower buds. Wattles are another favourite possum food, especially in winter. My mother has fed a family of possums for about ten years and they now eat leftover bits of fruit and bread dipped in honey straight from her hand.

Today koalas are unlikely to be sighted in urban areas, though they may be found often in eucalyptus-rich areas at the headwaters of streams and river systems. It is imperative that koalas have an adequate supply of fresh food leaves and they only eat the new growth of species such as the grey gum (*Eucalyptus*

punctata) and the forest red gum (*E. tereticornis*). They are solitary animals and make astonishingly fearsome growling noises to ward off intruders.

Those other native animals so strongly associated with the Australian heritage, kangaroos, wallabies and wombats, are unlikely to venture into highly developed areas either, but are to be found quite often in and around regional towns. Kangaroos and wallabies are essentially grazing animals, feeding on grasses, herbs and, in the case of the swamp wallaby, leaves of trees and shrubs. Apart from being illegal, it is also rather cruel to keep wombats, kangaroos or wallabies away from their natural habitat, so if one happens to venture into your garden, rather than encouraging it to stay by feeding them, you should ask the National Parks and Wildlife Service in your state to take them back to a shelter or to the bush, if possible.

Bats often form camps in remnant bushland, even in quite built-up areas. One quite famous colony has thrived for many years in Sydney's Centennial Park, right in the middle of the busy city. Bats are the only mammals capable of sustained flight. Flying-foxes and fruit bats, characterised by large eyes and an almost dog-like snout, feed on pollen, fruit and nectar. One of the most common is the grey-headed flying-fox, which loves to eat eucalyptus blossoms as well as the fruit of the Moreton Bay fig tree. Other bats, including the sheathtail and freetail, are mainly insectivorous, snacking on caterpillars, cockroaches, moths and flying or aquatic insects.

Rather than being seen as evil, blood-sucking creatures, bats in general are enjoying a resurgence in popularity in urban areas as people realise their importance in the ecosystem — fruit bats and flying-foxes are important seed dispersers and pollinators and the insectivorous bats help control insects that could otherwise damage parkland. The Wildlife Information and Rescue Service (WIRES) has popularised the idea of families 'adopting' baby bats which might otherwise perish, thus helping to build up the numbers in the colonies again. The mature bats are then released into bushland with safety.

Many reptiles can be found lurking around the family garden. The most diverse — and often the most beautiful — group is the skinks. The smaller and more agile ones are largely insectivorous, while the larger ones feed on berries, fruit and snails. Probably the most commonly known large skink is the dear old blue tongue lizard. There are several varieties: the blotched blue tongue, the stumpytail or shingleback and the striped eastern blue tongue. They often seek shelter under stacked firewood and in rockeries. Ours lives very happily behind the compost bin, alternatively sunning himself and eating — what a life! Sadly, blue tongues are often mistakenly killed because their head looks like that of a snake. Others meet an untimely death via snail pellets or a neighbourhood dog. They really are very mild creatures and help in the garden, eating many snails and spiders, so if you find one, do try to keep it safe. Blue tongue lizards are harmless, but can inflict a painful bite should you be foolish enough to put a finger in their mouth.

The fence skink is another suburban garden favourite, so named — you guessed it — because it is most often seen scampering along a wooden paling fence or brick wall. These are the tiny (to 15 centimetres) brown skinks with two cream stripes down their back, which will drop their tails if frightened or threatened. Some geckoes, notably the southern leaf-tailed gecko and the thick-tailed gecko, will set up home in urban areas, finding shelter in brick piles and under garden pots. They are more common in tropical areas. Like skinks, geckoes will drop their tails if molested but there the similarities end. Their bodies usually have a rough, spiky appearance and some may cough or 'bark' if frightened.

Probably the most dramatic type of lizard to find in your garden is the eastern water dragon. One specimen has been recorded as being over 1.2 metres long! More usually they are about 30 centimetres long and are distinguished by a crest of spines running all the way down their back. When challenged, they will attack, inflating their throat pouches to increase their apparent size and, hopefully, frighten you. However, they are not aggressive by nature; rather like the blue tongue, they would far prefer to bask on a log or rock all day long or drop into water for a swim.

They are usually found near freshwater streams and rivers and will patronise a quiet backyard fish pond. Brackish coastal waters and mangrove flats are also home to water dragons.

Goannas, on the other hand, tend to use their well-developed claws and teeth to attack quite readily if they are disturbed and can inflict a painful injury. Goannas are fast and agile lizards, and are distinguished by having a forked tongue. Some species can grow up to 2 metres long. It is only rarely encountered in urban areas and should really be given a very wide berth, especially where children are involved.

Similarly, unless you have a comprehensive knowledge of the different types of snakes, it is best to stay right away from these, too. Of the approximately 130 species of snakes in Australia, nearly half are poisonous. Species such as the tiger snake, death adder, copperhead, eastern small-eyed snake and eastern brown snake rank among the world's deadliest. Some, like the yellow-eyed whip snake and the swamp snake, are venomous but not necessarily dangerous, meaning they can inflict a painful bite, but not kill. Should you wish to identify any species you see in the bush or in your own garden, an excellent reference text is *Reptiles* by Ken Griffiths (Three Sisters Productions, 1987). If you are concerned about a snake, the National Parks and Wildlife Service will send a herpetologist to your home who will, if necessary, trap the snake and take it back to the bush. *Do not* try to do this yourself — most people are only bitten by snakes when they are trying to catch them or kill them.

By the same token, give spiders a wide berth. The most widespread ones, such as the huntsman and St Andrew's cross, are quite harmless and are in fact very useful as fly catchers, but trapdoors and funnel web spiders should be treated with the utmost caution. With any spider bite, go as quickly as possible to the nearest hosptial. (Do not squash the spider, as it may be needed for identification for an anti-venene, if necessary.) In dry periods, funnel webs have been known to fall into swimming pools, however, they should never be handled as they are known to be able to survive for a considerable period underwater. In short, treat all native animals which might appear in your garden with respect.

Frogs are another group of animals that are widely found in suburban areas. You can boost the numbers of frogs in your area by providing a few shady, moist sections planted with ferns or mosses, or even a garden pond. We were delighted to find a few of the pretty little dwarf tree frogs (only 4 centimetres long) in our front garden where they have made their home in a fine thick *Genista* or broom which, in turn, is next to the water tap and therefore usually slightly boggy. They can create a surprisingly loud chorus at dusk. Other frogs you may find visiting your garden are the striped marsh frog, the common eastern tree frog, barred frogs and the green tree frogs.

As a general rule, frogs are most active during warmer weather, becoming dormant in winter. Frogs living in trees tend to be a bright green, whereas their ground-dwelling cousins are more likely to be brown or a blotchy grey to better camouflage themselves. Tree frogs require water to breed and can sometimes be found in a damp cellar or garage.

What would the Australian summer be without the earsplitting din of cicadas? I really know hot days have arrived when I hear cicadas drumming away in the morning — and you certainly cannot ignore the noise they make when they are in full voice! The most common is the brightly coloured greengrocer, followed by the black prince and the cherrynose, with its cute, clownlike face. Rarer species include the red eyes, double drummers, squeakers and floury bakers.

Safety Tip

When mowing the lawn, keep any toddlers well away. A pebble can easily fly up and catch them unawares giving them at best, a nasty fright.

The kookaburra is often a familiar sight in the suburban garden

Attracting Birds and Insects

Birds contribute greatly to pest control in gardens and, therefore, reduce the necessity for using many chemical controls which may be toxic to pets or children, not to mention to the birds you are trying to attract to your garden in the first place. As a general warning, only sprays which are environmentally safe, such as pyrethrum, should be used in the family garden. White oil will control many common infestations, such as scale and sooty mould, without proving fatal to birds and wild animals or domestic pets.

To attract birds, a family garden must provide a desirable environment in which they may live and feed. Food, water, protective cover and a sheltered place to raise their young are the basic elements. Also, many plants will attract birds, whether they are coming to eat the particular nectar or seeds, or to snack on certain insects which also like that species. Each season offers certain inducements to birds, but a plant that flowers right throughout the year is probably the most attractive.

Nectar-filled native plants like kangaroo paw and *Grevillea* 'Robyn Gordon' will attract native birds. Attractive plants like buddleia and *Psoralea* will attract birds as well as insects, notably butterflies (see page 152). Parrots like sunflower seeds or seeds with 'fluffy' seed heads; finches will eat grass seeds and millet, while pigeons and doves like wheat. (Of course, some birds, such as kookaburras, like to eat meat. It is a simple matter to ask your butcher for half a kilogram of cheap chopped meat scraps, but I do not really like the idea of having raw meat in the family backyard. There is always a chance that a child could pick up a forgotten piece that has spoiled lying in the sun.)

As a general rule, plan to introduce plants that will provide as great a mixture of food as possible: grasses, grains, cones, berries and nuts. Select plants that will bear food in different seasons and do not prune the plants too closely; a lot of birds prefer shaded areas. Many nurseries now tag plants that will attract birds.

Do not root up all the weeds in the garden, leave a section wild to give cover for birds and to attract the insects to whom weeds are both home and pantry. Both ladybirds and their grubs have enormous appetites for aphids and other garden pests a single ladybird can eat about 50 aphids a day. However, you may have difficulty convincing the neighbours that attracting aphids to your family's garden is a good thing.

Understanding the role that insects play in the garden is an important way for children to learn about the complex web of life: aphids feed on roses, ladybirds eat aphids, birds eat ladybirds, and if you use poisonous sprays to kill the aphids, you will also harm or kill the other members of your backyard ecosystem.

Prickly plants, such as *Hakea suaveolens,* discourage dogs and cats and provide safe nesting sites for birds. Naturally, it is wise to teach children from their earliest years that thorns and prickles will hurt and they should leave such shrubs alone. Similarly, dense-growing or fine-leafed trees and shrubs provide excellent thickets for screening and for bird-nesting habitats. A wire fence can be hidden with a range of densely foliaged shrubs and vines which, in a very short time, will hide the fence completely. Wire mesh nailed to both sides of wooden uprights will soon form a 'double' fence and a quick-growing tangle of climbing plants will soon provide a safe and protected nesting site for birds. Remember that an irregularly constructed fence is more interesting and can make a piece of land seem wider. A double fence, as described above, could be taken around an existing tree or shrub if necessary, providing two possible nesting sites for birds.

When planning the layout of your family's garden, try to incorporate plants of varying height; the effect is more likely to resemble the birds' natural habitat. Shrubs and evergreens provide much-needed middle height cover for birds; try to situate them close to the birds' food and water sources. Try to provide a resource the

In the colder months, pyracantha berries can provide much needed food for birds

or two insects. Birds will often fly many kilometres to obtain water and species that would not otherwise venture into a backyard may be tempted if there is water. Bathing is part of a bird's intricate grooming behaviour that helps to keep its feathers clean, water-proofed and in good working order. After bathing, most will seek out a sunny perch on which to preen. It is imperative that this perch does not offer deadly opportunities for a neighbourhood cat wet wings do not flap quite as well as dry ones, making birds very vulnerable after their bath. For preference, set your birdbath in an open spot beneath an overhanging branch.

birds need that they may have trouble finding anywhere else. For instance, if most local trees are deciduous, plant one or two evergreens; cone-bearing evergreens will attract finches. Or, consider planting a pyracantha or other type of bush that holds its berries in the cold months so the birds do not have to forage elsewhere during winter. This is important because winter feeding actually attracts more birds than summer feeding. In the summertime, most garden birds disperse to establish nesting territories but in winter, many insects become dormant and are unavailable as food. Also, birds must eat large amounts of food in winter just to keep warm. One word of warning: if you plan to feed the birds through winter, be sure to be consistent. This is especially true during very bad weather when birds that have learned to come to your garden may not locate a new source of food quickly enough to stay alive.

Birds love to splash and bathe in shallow water. When you think about it, obtaining clean fresh water every day is probably a more difficult task for a bird than catching one

Safety Tip

Never leave water in a paddle pool or wading pool. Empty the pool and either deflate it or store it upside-down or standing against a wall.

Many quite beautiful birdbaths may be purchased through garden centres, creating an aesthetically pleasing accent for the garden as well as a practical one. There is a wide variety of styles and shapes, including one-piece terracotta or plastic birdbaths which fit directly into the soil as well as more ornate concrete, terracotta and plastic standard birdbaths or hanging wooden, terracotta or glazed ceramic birdbaths.

Simplest of all is the homemade birdbath; consider the potential of a rock containing a natural depression, a ceramic saucer on top of a tree stump, or even a humble garbage tin lid, upturned on a log or set in the ground. However, just like children, birds are contrary creatures and may boycott your birdbath if it is in too exposed a position, patronising instead a sunwarmed puddle in a rock depression in your rockery. Even if you have not built a rockery, search for a suitable rock and position it near a tap or sandy, sunny outcrop where you can enjoy watching the birds drink and splash.

Even in the most confined spaces, where only a balcony or window ledge is available, it is possible to attract birds to bathe and drink in a bowl. A tip to remember: fill the bowl regularly with fresh water and angle a branch or twig (a wooden ruler is just right) into the water so the birds may use it as a perch. Some birds like to duck themselves completely but smaller ones, such as honeyeaters, will be frightened by too much water. They prefer to stand in very shallow water and scoop it up with the wings, splashing it on themselves. In the family garden, small bowls can be positioned in several different areas, preferably near or just partially under thick shrubbery or ferns so that birds have somewhere to retreat to if confronted by a cat.

A wide variety of terracotta or ceramic bowls are available, or you might like to try your hand at making a very simple one, using a light cement mix with a little soil added for colour, or even shredded pine bark or leaf mulch. The mixture should neither crumble (indicating it is too dry) nor slump (indicating it is too wet). If you have purchased pre-mixed concrete for a path or a courtyard area, then it is a simple matter to experiment with the leftovers. Heap up a 'mould', using slightly dampened sand to about 10 centimetres high, on a potter's board and then, using a spatula, shape your bowl evenly around it. Of course, any chips or discolourations will only add to the rustic appeal. Do not place shallow bowls of water around the garden if any of your children are under four years of age.

Birdseed is the mainstay of any bird-attracting program. It is fairly inexpensive, especially if bought in large quantities, easy to store and convenient to use. At any pet supply store you can purchase seed bells or seed balls and hang them in the trees for the birds. You could also make or adapt a simple, tray-like feeder and fill it with a mixture of bread, honey and water. Experiment with different spots for your feeder or feeding tray before choosing one. Birds like their food sources to be predictable so, once you find locations that work, stick to them. Many birds like to dart quickly to a tray or seed ball, nip a few seeds and retreat to the safety of a bush or hedge so, as with the birdbath, it is best to situate a bird feeder within easy reach of shelter. Large tree trunks and leafy shrubs provide sheltered areas. This is particularly important for tray feeders as the extra shelter reduces the likelihood of the seed being blown over the garden.

There are also many bird houses sold commercially, scaled to suit different types of birds, which can be put into trees to attract them. Bird houses can be decorative or whimsical, but they must also be functional. They need the capacity to hold bird seed, a platform on which birds may alight and a sheltered nesting area. I am very fond of the once old-fashioned now new again pigeon houses — the chalet style with a shingle roof and a multitude of windows. Wild birds do not seem to like these so much but pigeons and doves will make themselves right at home. Also, before becoming enthusiastic about installing a dovecote or an aviary, be sure to check with the authorities and the neighbours. In some closely settled areas certain birds, notably poultry, are banned and in other areas certain exotic species (not indigenous ones) are banned. Also remember neighbours are seldom as enthusiastic about birds as their owners are and will be unlikely to appreciate a large aviary being sited along a boundary fence.

BIRD-ATTRACTING PLANTS

WATER PLANTS

Banksia robur

Callistemon speciosus

SHRUBS

Acacia triptera

Bauhinia carronii

Beaufortia macrostemon

Calothamnus spp.

Correa spp.

Grevillea spp. (especially those with red or pink flowers)

Hakea bucculenta

Hakea verrucosa

Kunzea baxteri

Lambertia ericifolia

Melaleuca coccinea

Melaleuca macronycha

Telopea spp.

TREES

Callistemon salignus

Eucalyptus spp. (hollow branches provide excellent nesting sites, especially for parrots)

Olea paniculata

Syzygium leuhmannii

Syzygium moorei

Syzygium paniculatum

CLIMBERS

Agapetes meiniana

APPENDIX

WHAT NOT TO PLANT
Poisonous Plants

Many parents have no idea just how poisonous many common garden plants are. Up to five per cent of poisonings each year are due to plants, excluding mushrooms. Although many plant poisonings are relatively insignificant, for example, a rash caused by skin contact with sap or outer plant parts such as leaves and stems, occasionally far more serious results can occur.

Poisonous plants should not be planted in or near children's play areas. It is also wise to be aware of those plants which, while not actually poisonous, produce illness, allergy, or irritation. Plant-induced dermatitis or hayfever are often allergic reactions in a sensitive child. The best way to relieve stinging is to liberally dab the affected area with antihistamine lotion. However, the spines, prickles, and thorns of some plants also will not only puncture the skin but can inject poisons. Pampas grass (*Cortaderia* spp.) while not poisonous, has very sharp leaves which can result in a vicious cut. Other common plants which are known to cause dermatitis include:

Buttercup, leaves (*Ranunculus* spp.)
Century plant (*Agave* spp.)
Chrysanthemum daisy, leaves
(*Chrysanthemum* spp.)
Dock or sorrel, leaves (*Rumex* spp.)
English box, leaves (*Buxus sempervirens*)
Frangipani, sap (*Plumeria* spp.)
Grevillea, all parts (*Grevillea banksii*)
Hellebore, leaves (*Veratrum* spp.)
Iris, roots (*Iris* spp.)
Ivy, leaves (*Hedera helix*)
Larkspur, leaves and seeds (*Delphinium* spp.)

Maidenhair tree, seeds (*Ginkgo biloba*)
Mulberry, leaves (*Morus rubra*)
Oleander, sap (*Nerium oleander*)
Plumbago, all parts (*Plumbago auriculata*)
Poinsettia, sap (*Euphorbia pulcherrima*)
Primula, leaves (*Primula* spp.)
Stinging nettle, hairs (*Urtica dioica*)

Many rhododendrons, oleanders and castor oil plants, the seeds of which are very toxic, seem to be widely planted in family gardens, hopefully without harm. And who would think that the gorgeous daffodil, greatly prized for its beauty and usefulness in landscaping, has a poisonous bulb? For my money, it is just not worth the risk nor the worry. I have a particularly pretty flurry of potato vine (*Solanum* spp.) all down one fence and I admit to being in two minds about ripping it out when it is so lovely, but its days are numbered now that Randall is crawling about and putting everything into his mouth.

It would be almost impossible to ban every plant which is inedible or even irritating to the skin. Moreover, many such plants have value as natural insecticides when used carefully in gardens. Adults also need to realise that children see and think about things differently. It would not occur to an adult to try and eat a peach stone, they would eat only the flesh. Yet the seeds inside peach stones are almost identical in appearance to almonds, so a child could easily reason that they were indeed the same, but with terrible results, as the stones contain cyanic acid. It is best to teach children from their earliest years never to eat any part of any plant not known to be safe. Caution the child old enough to understand about eating wild berries or fruits or chewing on bark or stems. Watch younger children in the garden, just as you would watch them and keep them from running into the street. Fortunately, most poisonous plants have an unpleasant taste and a child is likely to spit them out.

Two other safety tips: pull up *any* mushrooms or toadstools as soon as they appear, and bury any animal excreta before your child has a chance to poke at it, play with it, or even eat it. In the case of an emergency where you suspect a child has been poisoned by eating a dangerous plant or plant part, induce vomiting if the child is conscious. This may be done by giving him or her a tablespoon of salt in a glass of warm water or a dose of Ipecac syrup — always keep a bottle in the medicine chest. Only attempt to give the child a drink if he or she is conscious; if they are not, they may well choke on the liquid. Keep the patient warm and use artificial respiration if they are not breathing. Telephone your doctor immediately and ask for an ambulance to come and take the child to the closest hospital. An ambulance will be better equipped to keep the patient warm, still and lying down, rather than you trying to move them and sit them up in the family car. The telephone number across Australia for all enquiries to the Poisons Information Centre is (02) 692 6111.

INDOOR PLANTS

Caladium
Dieffenbachia
Elephant's Ear
Philodendron

GARDEN PLANTS AND SHRUBS

Almond
Amaryllis, naked lady (*Brunsvigia rosea*) bulbs
Anemone (Pasque flower) young plants, flowers
Angel's trumpet, thorn apple, jimsonweed (*Datura* spp.), all parts
Apple (*Malus* spp.) leaves and seeds

Apple of Sodom
Apricot, seeds
Arum lily
Asparagus (*Asparagus officinalis*), young unripe stems
Autumn crocus, meadow saffron (*Colchimum autumnale*), leaves
Azalea (*Rhododendron* spp.), all parts

Begonia, leaves
Belladonna lily (*Amaryllis belladonna*), bulbs
Bermuda buttercup (*Oxalis cernua*), leaves
Bird of Paradise (*Poinciana gilliesii*), pods and seeds
Black locus (*Robinia pseudoacacia*), young shoots, bark and seeds
Black nightshade (*Solanum nigrum*), green berries
Black snakeroot (*Zigadenus*), bulbs and flowers
Bleeding heart, all parts
Blood root (*Sanguinaria canadensis*), flower and sap
Box (*Buxus sempervirens*), leaves
Broom (*Cytisus* spp.), seeds
Bushman's poison (*Acokanthera* spp.), all parts
Buttercup (*Ranunculus* spp.), leaves
Button bush (*Cephalanthus occidentalis*), leaves

Caladium, leaves
Canary bird bush (*Crotalaria* spp.), seeds
Castor oil plant (*Ricinus communis*), whole plant
Catnip (*Nepeta cataria*), seeds
Cestrum, night blooming jasmine (*Cestrum* spp.), leafy shoots
Cherries, peaches and plums (*Prunus* spp.), seeds and leaves
Chinaberry (*Melia azedarach*), fruit, flowers and bark
Christmas berry (*Photinia arbutifolia*), leaves
Christmas rose (*Helleborus niger*), rootstocks and leaves
Clematis (*Clematis vitalba*), leaves
Climbing lily (*Gloriosa* spp.), all parts
Coffee berry, buckthorn (*Rhamnus* spp.), sap and fruit
Columbine (*Aquilegia vulgaris*), seeds
Coral tree (*Erythrina* spp.), seeds

Cotoneaster, berries

Cow parsnip (*Heracleum lanatum*), leaves and
    roots

Crepe jasmine

Crinum lily (*Crinum asiaticum*), bulbs

Culvers root (*Veronica virginica*), roots

Cunjevoi (*Alocasia*)

Daffodil (*Narcissus* spp. and cvs.), bulbs

Daphne (*Daphne* spp.), bark, leaves and fruit

Deadly nightshade (*Solanum dulcamara*), sprouts
    and berries

Desert marigold (*Baileya multiradiata*), whole plant

Dumb cane (*Dieffenbachia seguine*), stems and
    leaves

Dutchman's breeches, bleeding heart
    (*Dicentra* spp.), leaves and tubers

Elder (*Sambucus* spp.), berries and flowers

Elderberry (*Sambucus vaccaria*), seeds

English holly (*Ilex aquifolium*), berries

European burning bush (*Euonymus europaea*),
    leaves and fruit

False morel (*Gyromita esculenta*), mushroom

Figs (*Ficus* spp.), milky sap

Firethorn (*Pyracantha* spp.), berries

Flax (*Linum halimifolium*), leaves and young
    shoots

Foxglove (*Digitalis purpurea*), leaves and flowers

Garden nightshade (*Solanum nigrum*), unripe
    berries and stems

German ivy (*Senecio mikanioides*), leaves and stems

Gingko, maidenhair tree (*Ginkgo biloba*), fruit
    juice

Gladioli (*Gladiolus* spp.), corm

Glory lily

Golden chain (*Laburnum vulgare*), leaves and
    seeds

Golden dewdrop (*Duranta erecta*), fruits and
    leaves

Ground ivy (*Nepeta hederacea*), leaves and stems

Hemlock (*Conium maculatum*), all parts

Henbane

Holly (*Ilex aquifolium*), berries

Horse chestnut/buck eye (*Aesculus* spp.), leaves
    and fruit

Hyacinth (*Hyacinthus* spp.), bulbs

Hydrangea (*Hydrangea macrophylla*), leaves and
    buds

Impatiens (*Impatiens* spp.), young stems and leaves

Irises (*Iris innominata, I. douglasiana, I. cristata,
    I. missouriensis*), roots

Ivy (*Hedera helix*), berries and leaves

Jack in the pulpit (*Arisaema triphyllum*), all parts,
    especially roots

Jade plant (*Crassula argentea*), leaves

Jerusalem cherry (*Solanum pseudocapsicum*), fruit

Jessamine (*Jasminum* spp.), berries

Karaka nut (*Corynocarpus laevigata*), seeds

Laburnum

Ladyslipper orchid (*Cypripedium* spp.), stems
    and leaves

Lantana (*Lantana* spp.), foliage and green berries

Larkspur, delphinium (*Delphinium* spp.), young
    plants and seeds

Laurel (*Laurus* spp.), all parts

Lily of the valley (*Convallaria majalis*), leaves
    and flowers

Lobelia

Loquat, seeds

Lupin

Marsh cowslip (*Caltha palustris*), all parts

Mayapple or mandrake (*Podophyllum peltatum*),
    fruit

Milkweed (*Asclepias* spp.), all parts

Mimosa tree (*Mimosa* spp.), seeds

Mistletoe (*Phoradendron* spp.), berries

Monkshood (*Aconitum* spp.), all parts

Moon flower (*Calonyction* spp.), seeds

Moonseed (*Menispermum*), berries

Moreton Bay chestnut (*Castanospermum
    australe*), seeds

Morning glory (*Ipomoea* spp.), seeds

Mountain laurel (*Kalmia latifolia*), leaves

Narcissus, daffodil (*Narcissus* spp.), bulbs

Nettle (*Urtica dioica*), leaves, stems and roots
Ngaio (*Myoporum laetum*), leaves
Nightshade (*Solanum* spp.), all parts

Oak (*Quercus* spp.), foliage and acorns
Oleander, (*Nerium oleander*) fruits, seeds and leaves
Opium poppy (*Papaver somniferum*), unripe seed pod

Parsnip (*Pastinaca sativa*), hairs on leaves and stems
Peach, kernels, flowers, leaves and bark
Pear, seeds
Philodendron (*Philodendron* spp.), stems and leaves
Pittosporum (*Pittosporum* spp.), leaves and stems
Poinsettia (*Euphorbia pulcherrima*), leaves and sap
Poison ivy
Potato (*Solanum tuberosum*), stems, rotten or green parts, leaves
Privet (*Ligustrum* spp.), leaves and berries

Queensland nut (*Macadamia ternifolia*), young leaves
Quince, seeds and fresh leaves

Ragwort (*Senecio* spp.), seeds
Rhododendron, azalea (*Rhododendron* spp.), all parts
Rhubarb (*Rheum rhaponticum*), leaves
Rhus tree/wax tree
Rosary pea (*Abrus precatorius*), seeds
Snapdragon (*Antirrhinum* spp.), leaves

Snowdrop
Sour dock (*Rumex acetosa*), leaves
Spider lily (*Hymenocallis americana*), bulbs
St. John's wort (*Hypericum perforatum*), all parts
Star of Bethlehem (*Ornithogalum umbellatum*), all parts
Summer adonis (*Adonis aestivalis*), leaves and stems
Sweet pea

Tansy (*Tanacetum vulgare*), leaves
Tobacco plants (*Nicotiana* spp.), foliage
Tomato, leaves
Tree of heaven (*Ailanthus altissima*), leaves and flowers
Tulip (*Tulipa* spp.), bulb

Walnut (*Juglans* spp.), green hull juice
Water hemlock (*Cicuta* spp.), all parts
White cedar (*Melia azedarach*), berries and leaves
White snakeroot (*Eupatorium rugosum*), leaves and stems
Wintersweet
Wisteria (*Wisteria* spp.), all parts

Yellow jessamine (*Gelsemium sempervirens*), flowers, leaves and roots
Yew (*Taxus baccata*), foliage, bark and seeds

Zephyr lily (*Zephyranthes* spp.), leaves and bulbs

For further information, the following should be available through libraries or book suppliers:

Poisonous Plants of Australia, Selwyn L. Everist; Angus & Robertson Australia, 1974

BIBLIOGRAPHY

Aikman, A., *Treehouses;* Robert Hale, London 1988

Better Homes and Gardens' Flower Arranging Book; Meredith Publishing Co, 1957

Bjork, C. and Anderson, L., *Linnaeas' Windowsill Gardening;* R & S Books/Farrar, Strauss & Girous, New York 1978

Burke, D., *Burke's Backyard;* Hutchinson Australia/Margaret Gee, 1989

Burke, D., *Burke's Backyard Information Guide;* Hutchinson/Margaret Gee, Australia 1989

Clifton, C., *Edible Flowers;* The Bodley Head, London 1983

Clyne, D., *How to Attract Butterflies to Your Garden;* Reed Books, Sydney, Australia 1990

Crush, M., *Gardening Outdoors;* Franklin Watts, London 1973

Dutton, N., *Presents from your Garden;* Nelson, Australia 1986

Fletcher, K., *Australian Herbal Crafts;* Penguin Books, Australia 1992

Fletcher, K., *Herbal Crafts;* Greenhouse/Penguin, Australia 1992

Flowers and Plants in the Home; Marshall Cavendish Ltd, London 1973

Gadd, L., *Deadly Beautiful;* Macmillan Publishing Co Inc, New York 1980

Gordon, L., *Green Magic;* Ebury Press/Webb and Bower, London 1977

Griffiths, K., *Reptiles;* Three Sisters Productions, Australia 1987

Hargreaves B., *Handbook of Country Crafts;* Drive Publications Ltd, London 1973

Heinz, K., *How does your Garden Grow?;* The Five Mile Press, Australia 1985

Hemphill, E., *Your First Book of Herb Gardening;* Angus & Robertson, Australia 1980

Horne, D.E., *Trampolining;* Faber & Faber, London 1978

Ingram, A. and O'Donnell, P., *Out in the Garden;* Ellsyd Press, Australia 1990

La Barge, L., *The Pet House Book;* Butterick Publishing, New York 1977

Lancashire, D., *Gardening — How to Grow Things;* Kestrel Books, McPhee Gribble, Melbourne 1976

Lawrence, M. (ed) *Garden Brickwork;* New Holland Publishers, London 1988

McKinlay, I., *Gardening for Kids;* Collins Dove, Australia 1979

Meyers, J., *Make the Most of Your Lawn;* Hart Publishing Inc., New York 1978

Moddy, M. and Maddocks, C., *The Potted Garden;* Bucks Books/Horowitz Group Books, Australia 1979

Newcomb, D., *The Postage Stamp Garden Book;* Horwitz Publications/Castle Books, Hong Kong 1978

Outdoor Playhouses and Toys, Workbench Magazine/*Modern Handcraft;* Sterling Publishing Co Inc, New York 1985

Pastorelli, J. (ed) *Urban Wildlife;* Angus & Robertson, Australia 1990

Pavord, A., *Growing Things;* Macmillan Publishers, London 1982

Pfeiffer, A., *Australian Garden Design;* Macmillan Australia, Melbourne 1983

Pienaar, K. and Greig, D., *What to Plant? — An Illustrated Guide for Australian Gardens;* Angus & Robertson (no date given)

Powell, C., *The Meaning of Flowers;* Jupiter Books, London 1977

Reader's Digest How To Do Just About Anything; Reader's Digest, Australia 1987

Readers' Digest Compete Book of the Garden; The Reader's Digest Asscn Ltd, Australia 1967

Rees, Y., *The Art of Balcony Gardening;* Ward Lock, London 1991

Rix, M., *Window Boxes and Pots;* Penguin Books, London 1985

Roberts, J., *What Food is That?;* Weldon Publishing, Australia 1990

Rogers, S., *The Cook's Garden;* Collins Angus & Robertson, Australia 1992

Root, W., *Food — A Fireside Book;* Simon & Schuster Inc, New York 1980

Russell, R., *Spotlight on Possums;* University of Queensland Press, Queensland 1980

Rutherford, D. (ed) *Swimming Pools;* Sunset Books, Lane Publishing, California 1986

Schultz, N., *Backyard Games;* Grosset & Dunlap, New York 1975

Self, C.R., *Making Fancy Birdhouses and Feeders;* Sterling Publishing Co, New York 1988

Stevenson, B. (ed) *Stevenson's Book of Quotations,* (10th edn); Cassell, London 1934

Sutherland, Dr. S.K., *Venomous Creatures of Australia;* Oxford University Press, Melbourne 1981

Swift, L., *Flower Arranging;* Fawcett Publications, New York 1954

The Complete Works of William Shakespeare; Abbey Library/Murrays Sales, London 1974

The Oxford Dictionary of Quotations (2nd edn); Oxford University Press, London 1953

The Readers Digest Family Book of Things to Make and Do; Readers Digest Asscn, London 1977

Thisleton-Dyer, T.F., *The Folklore of Plants;* Chatto & Windus, London 1889

Victorian Department of Youth, Sport and Recreation, Australia, *Life Be In It Games Manual;* Ashton Scholastic/Budget Books Pty Ltd, Australia 1980

Walden, H., *Flowerworks;* Simon & Schuster, Australia 1987

Williams, P., *A Kid's Guide to Cubby Houses;* Hodder & Stoughton, Australia 1991

Wise, T., *Gardens for Children;* Kangaroo Press, Australia 1986

Worrell, E., *Things That Sting;* Angus & Robertson, Australia 1977

INDEX